July 2nd '79

Sarah

With love from Granny.

Improving Your Riding

David Tamplin

Peace of Mind

IMPROVING YOUR RIDING

An Introduction to
More Advanced Equitation

JANET HOLYOAKE

Photographic studies by
RICHARD HAMMONDS
and
DAVID TAMPLIN

FABER AND FABER
3 Queen Square
London

First published in 1966
by Faber and Faber Limited
3 Queen Square London WC1
New edition 1971
Reprinted 1972
Printed in Great Britain
by Latimer Trend & Co Ltd Plymouth

ISBN 0 571 04742 4

Drawings and Decorations
by
PHILLIPA GWYNNE JAMES

This book is dedicated to the many horses and ponies who long to be a little more expertly and COMFORTABLY ridden.

And who would only too thankfully be more co-operative if they could but fathom what their riders were driving at!

Immeasurable thanks are due to Mrs. Lorna Johnstone for her selfless kindness, encouragement, patience and inspiration to so many of us, for so long, in all matters appertaining to Dressage.

Also to Miss Rita Paske for helpfully participating in the photographs and for kindly permitting her beautiful Thoroughbred to pose for the camera.

Contents

Illustrations

LINE DIAGRAMS

PLATES

9

Illustrations

YOUR LESSONS

In this story you will see how Pippa was able to teach an old horse, who had been given to her and was inclined to be rather unmanageable, to mend his ways despite his advanced years and become a tractable and suitable mount for her, as well as a very dear friend.

But in order to be able to get him to reform—or to re-school him as it is called—she soon found that it was SHE, HERSELF *who must first* IMPROVE HER OWN RIDING.

It is just possible that your riding also may leave much to be desired! So in case you too might like to try to improve, the same instruction that was given to Pippa is set out in simple, abbreviated form for you in 'YOUR LESSONS'.

Study them carefully. Follow the advice if you can. Try it all out for yourself.
And see what happens!

Introduction

Peter was a gift horse, and as everyone knows, one should never look a gift horse in the mouth. But Pippa had no need to pry inquisitively and ungraciously at Peter's teeth, for the Master of Hounds who gave him to her, made no bones about Peter's age. Peter was eighteen years old if he was a day, he told Pippa candidly, and though still sound in wind and limb, his years were beginning to take their toll and he could no longer stand up to a hard day's hunting. So the place in the Hunt Stables that Peter had gallantly filled for many a season must regretfully be vacated in favour of younger blood. So it came about that he was offered as a gift to Pippa on the strict understanding that hers was to be his final home.

Pippa was entranced. Her parents' purse was far from bottomless and she knew full well that the chance of having a horse of her own would never come again. So come what might she was determined to accept this kindly offer, even though Peter might hardly perhaps appear to be an ideal mount for her.

But Pippa's parents were a little less enthusiastic. Indeed they were singularly dubious. Pippa was a slip of a girl and Peter a large and strongly built horse and as the Huntsman cheerfully warned them he was hard, if not impossible, to stop once he got going and quite impossible to catch once he was turned out! Indeed, when running out in summer a rare old rascal was he; not above chasing sheep and even (so it was whispered) had been known to make short work of a lamb or two. But he was a grand old horse for all his faults; never sick nor sorry; always game to face up to any obstacle; always ready to go—even if not quite so willing to stop!—so who could blame him if he turned a bit awkward at times?

At this recital of Peter's misdeeds, Pippa's parents' concern mounted rapidly, but she herself became more determined than ever to accept this kindly offer and have Peter for her very own. Perhaps he would change his ways, she said.

So it happened that we were consulted and we felt very much inclined to agree with Pippa—perhaps Peter could be persuaded to change. For in our humble estimation no horse is too old to be taught, with patience and understanding, to alter his habits and outlook, to mend his ways, or to be reschooled, as it is called—provided, of course, THAT HE IS SOUND.

In Peter's case one could but try to see if he could be persuaded to become a somewhat more tractable and suitable mount for his young mistress. The experiment would certainly be an interesting one, and we suggested that perhaps the easiest way of carrying it out would be for Peter to come and stay with us for a time, while Pippa visited him as often as school time and studies would permit.

Perhaps you, too, have a horse whose manners are not all that they might be and who can, at times, be difficult to manage. Or perhaps you have a youngster coming along who needs to have finishing touches put to his education. If so, this true story of Peter and Pippa may possibly help and perhaps be an inspiration to you to try similar tactics.

To this end has this little book been written.

I · *Peace of Mind*

When, one bright morning at the Hunt Stables, the Huntsman proceeded to load Peter into the horsebox, familiar as was this event Peter had an instinctive sinking feeling that he was being loaded for the last time. He began to sweat profusely with apprehension as the horsebox swayed along. He did not feel at all inclined to change homes at his time of life and when, on arrival at their destination, he found himself confronted by a strange yard and unfamiliar stable, his worst fears were confirmed and he flatly refused to take one step into his new abode.

Poor Pippa, her heart sank. It seemed not a very good beginning.

But the Jovial Huntsman who had brought Peter was unabashed. He snatched up a stable bucket and got behind his reluctant charge . . . clatter . . . bang . . . wallop and 'In we go, old fellow!'

Peter had painful recollections of other unseemly arguments with the Huntsman and into the stable he charged with no further ado, nearly knocking over and flattening his apprehensive new owner whom the Huntsman advised to 'look slippy' and jump out of the light if she did not want her toes broken with Peter's large feet descending heavily upon hers. 'He's a big customer and you want to keep clear of his heels in the stable,' he warned ominously. 'But you'll get along fine, lass!' he predicted cheerfully. 'Just strap down his head tight mind, with a standing martingale, when you ride him. And take a good pull at the reins and he'll stop all right . . . when he WANTS to!' was the Jovial Huntsman's parting shot as he sped cheerfully on his way.

Pippa, for the first time, felt far from jovial. Her heart was rapidly descending into her boots. But we, strangely enough—as we gazed at Peter's wise old head as he stood there sweating and snorting, eyeing his new surroundings with deep suspicion—we felt strangely optimistic.

Obviously the first thing to be done was to settle him down happily in his new home and inspire confidence and peace of mind, for most of us who have taken even a passing interest in the subject of schooling, or re-schooling, must have read and heard scores of times such adages as . . . 'Horses, just like people, can never be persuaded to concentrate upon anything, certainly not to the extent of learning and absorbing new ways, unless they be calm, quiet and relaxed.' And this peace of mind must of necessity start in the stable.

So the very first step along the road to re-schooling Peter would have to be to work out a methodical, daily stable-routine programme and to make every effort to make him feel thoroughly at home, comfortable, happy and relaxed. On the whole, old horses seem to do best when kept on the Combined System—that is living in the stable by night and running out for a few hours by day. (You can read further details of this system in another little book—*Your Book on Keeping Ponies* written by the same author and produced by the same publisher.)

Under the Combined System Peter would be warmly and comfortably housed, which wards off many an ill in the elderly or 'aged', as old horses are always called. But even more important, he would have a quiet stable in which to relax and rest. For proper periods of absolute peace and rest are extremely important to the well-being of any horse and especially so to one who is going to be asked to absorb ideas which may be new and strange to him: who is in fact going to be re-schooled.

Another advantage of the Combined System would be that Peter would have regular meals. (Remember the Golden Rule that 'Little and Often' maintains, and puts on condition.) And not only would these regular meals help to get, and to keep him fit, and in a semi-hard condition, but they would also pleasantly divide the day and prevent boredom. (Satan finds plenty of mischief for idle horses to do, sheep-chasing and lamb-killing being by no means exceptional!) But with the Combined System, time spent out of doors is limited and every precious moment has to be devoted to grazing, leaving little to spare for such pranks. Yet these few hours spent daily in the fields would be just enough to give Peter the succulent, green food so essential to continued good health (Doctor Green is the best veterinary surgeon!), as well as providing the gentle exercise, the sunshine, the sense of freedom and the fresh air for which every animal craves and which should be his heritage.

'But how are we going to catch him again, if we once turn him out?' asked Pippa with some misgiving. When she had asked the Huntsman the same question he had laughed. 'Ask me another!' he chuckled. 'You will have to get your school friends to come along and round him up and drive him in!' he suggested.

But to depend upon the 'wild west' services of a horde of school friends seemed a somewhat impractical proposition. We suggested instead that the very first lesson that Peter should learn, must be to come when he was called.

'But that will take YEARS!' sighed poor Pippa. How surprised she was to find it only took a few days. Indeed, no precious time was lost in beginning this first and most essential lesson. Peter had to start learning it the day after his arrival.

We kept him in the stable for the first two days, for as everyone knows, and as Pippa could well guess, to have tried to turn him straight out into a new field whilst we ourselves were still strangers to him would indeed have been the height of folly. Up would have gone his tail in the air and off he would have set with a snort and a buck at full gallop round and round that new field working himself, as he tore round and round, into a frenzy of agitation and even terror in these unaccustomed surroundings; and what hope would we have then of getting anywhere near him? An unfortunate introduction to a new home, and one to be avoided at all costs.

So instead we kept him in for a couple of days and let him get used to us gradually, hoping that he would soon discover for himself that though pitched out from his old familiar home, suddenly and entirely without warning, nevertheless there was really no undue cause for alarm in this unexpected turn of events.

Pippa must help to calm his fears by paying him VERY FREQUENT visits and, whilst thus engaged, she must begin his first lesson.

Each time that Pippa visited him she must take a halter into the stable with her. We gave her an old halter that had become a little tattered but very soft with long usage and each time she visited Peter throughout the day she just put it on him. But this halter had to be put on with a difference, NOT JUST SLAMMED OVER HIS HEAD any old how. We showed Pippa instead how to hold it out ready (look at the picture) and standing fair and square, directly in front of Peter, she gradually persuaded him to DROP HIS HEAD and allow his nose to be guided into it. Then as soon as he had permitted the halter to be QUIETLY and GENTLY put over his head, he must be IMMEDIATELY rewarded—BUT NOT BEFORE.

(Again you may read about this simple method of teaching the 'un-catchable' to learn to be 'caught' in another little book—*Your Book on Keeping Ponies.*)

Then there was something else that Pippa was advised to remember each time that she visited Peter throughout that first day—and for many weeks and months afterwards—to be EXAGGERATEDLY QUIET and GENTLE in all her movements. Such gentleness, such quiet, calm movements, such care not to so much as ruffle his FEELINGS, much less barely dislodge a hair of his mane, such extreme consideration would be something even stranger to Peter than these new and unfamiliar surroundings. His long life had been spent in the service of the Hunt where no pains had been spared as far as his physical welfare was concerned to give him of the best. His corn and hay had always been of the finest quality that could be procured; his bed of the deepest and cleanest straw; his gruel, when he came home weary from a hard day's hunting, was well and carefully prepared; and his weekly bran mash made appetizing and tasty with all the necessary extra ingredients. If he had 'pulled out' a bit stiff or lame one morning, or when some minor mishap had rendered him temporarily unsound, he had been immediately rested; carefully nursed and duly cosseted; and veterinary aid was never begrudged nor lacking if and when it had been needed. And throughout the long summer months he had been turned out with his companions to spend idle days in good pasture for a much-needed and well-earned rest. Needless to say as a result of this experience and EXPERT care, Peter at the ripe old age of eighteen was still as sound as a bell in wind and limb and constitutionally in very fine fettle.

But though this expert thought and care had always been bestowed upon his health and general well being, there had been little time in the busy hustle and bustle of the Hunt Kennels to pay much attention to Peter's feelings! Life at times was of necessity somewhat rough and ready! All through the hunting season work was hard, hours long, and labour often short. As often as not when Huntsman and Whipper-In came home tired and hungry after a long day out, they had to strip off their coats, roll up their sleeves and turn groom and stableboy before they themselves could relax for a rest and a meal. Small wonder that sometimes tempers were short and attentions slapdash.

'Here's the gruel, and there's the oats. Take 'em or leave 'em! Git over there! Look sharp can't you! Wallop! Bang! Thud! . . .' were the actions and sentiments to which Peter had grown accustomed. And as often as not he too had felt hot, tired and VERY grumpy! You throw my oats at me! You slam down that bucket and splash me all over and make me jump! You prod me again with that pitchfork as you straighten my bed! You push me round and shout at me just when I want a bit of peace and quiet to eat my feed and I'll kick the life out of you. Peter would threaten with ears laid back and heel raised.

Seldom, if ever, had his dire threats been actually put into practice, for deep down Peter had a very kind heart, but in course of time he had acquired the art of looking extremely alarming and forbidding. Vast experience had taught him that tit for tat was the best line to take and life at the Hunt Kennels had left little time or opportunity for practising the finer points of etiquette or the giving and receiving of more delicate attentions!

But as we all know, rough ways are apt to beget rough horses and Peter had become no exception to this rule. He took his good living as a matter of course but he did not entirely appreciate the way his platter was served and when, at the end of his summer holiday, he saw his captors arriving in a band at the field to recapture him and his companions and drag them back to noise, bustle, clatter and hard work again, he decided that he quite definitely preferred the peace and quiet of the green fields and so would outwit them if he could. What a song and dance he led them when they tried to catch him, and when they did get within range he was not above turning round and warding them off as long as possible with his very large heels!

Now Pippa must change all this before we could even begin our daily routine stable programme of regular periods inside and out, much less attempt any further steps towards his re-education.

Pippa must try and explain to him that she hoped very soon to become his great friend and that far from wanting to chase after and grab him, she simply hoped to persuade HIM to come to HER BECAUSE HE HIMSELF WISHED TO DO SO (this, of course, being the only possible way of teaching a horse or pony to come when it is called). And Pippa must find some means of explaining this to Peter by dint of ACTIONS—his knowledge of human speech being strictly limited and not altogether helpful!

So Pippa started that very first day after Peter's arrival by paying frequent visits to his stable. So she went in SO QUIETLY; she spoke to him so SOFTLY; she held out the halter SO SLOWLY; she suggested that she might be permitted to guide his nose into it SO POLITELY; she put it over his ears (his very tender ears rendered extra sensitive by the not infrequent use of a twitch); she lifted the soft, old halter right over his ears without so much as touching them, SO CAREFULLY; and when all this had been safely accomplished (NEVER BEFORE) she offered him the tastiest of titbits SO KINDLY and GRACIOUSLY.

As Peter turned over this bit of toast in his mouth, at one and the same time he turned over some thoughts in his mind, not the least of which was one of great surprise! He was indeed very surprised, not only at finding himself at his time of life suddenly transplanted into a new home, but an even greater surprise, he was being treated in an entirely different manner from that to which he had always been accustomed.

This little slip of a girl creeping into his stable so quietly, talking to him so softly and reassuringly, and handling him with such slow, deliberate, gentle movements and yet with such quiet confidence what could it all mean? Peter was indeed quite taken aback. And horses taken by surprise are often horses quickly won and conquered, especially when the surprise be a pleasant one!

So in one short day the first victory went to Pippa, for by the end of it Peter fully understood that when she came to visit him she wished him to STEP TOWARDS HER and obligingly LOWER HIS WISE OLD HEAD (instead of flinging it up and back and as far out of reach as possible as he was wont to do when approached by anything even faintly resembling a halter or a rope!). Instead, his new owner apparently wished him to DROP his head and PUT HIS NOSE INTO the outstretched halter. And as she was so QUIET, SO GENTLE, SO PATIENT and SO CAREFUL not to so much as ruffle his feelings, he felt very inclined—in view of the subsequent bit of toast—to comply with this simple request and do as he was asked.

'But what happens when we let him go in the field?' asked Pippa with some misgiving.

We would try the very next day to give her the answer. But just as an extra precautionary measure we would first introduce Peter to a suitable companion. Fortunately we still had Bronco with us. (Perhaps you have already met him through the pages of that other little book, *Your Book on Keeping Ponies*.)

Bronco is an ideal companion for all newcomers because he entirely ignores them! We put him in the stable next to Peter, and Peter, used for many a year by dint of size and strength to being 'Boss', lost no time in sniffing noses with Bronco through the bars and letting off the most blood-curdling squeals designed to turn the thickest blood to coldest water! But

Bronco was unimpressed. He turned his back upon Peter and his thoughts and attention to his hay, and Peter found it quite impossible to get any further reaction from him throughout the long night. Very disconcerting! But at the same time it was strangely comforting to a strange horse.

So when we ventured to turn Peter out the next morning into a very small paddock, he found Bronco already established in another little field alongside.

We did not, of course, attempt to turn them out together, for even though they appeared to have settled their differences very satisfactorily through the stable bars, to have turned them out together after only one short night of acquaintanceship would indeed have been the height of folly. For as most of us know already one should NEVER risk putting strange horses out together —more especially if they be shod—until they have had ample time and opportunity to dispense entirely with any suggestion of squeals and rude remarks over the fence! To do so sooner is simply to court disaster in the shape of kicks, quarrels and free fights ending almost certainly in damaged legs and in all probability an expensive visit from the vet—not to mention a couple of invalids on one's hands who will probably be 'un-rideable' for some considerable time to come.

Also, in Peter's case, to have turned him out with a companion ACTUALLY IN THE SAME FIELD would have helped to distract his attention (as well as give him a little undesirable moral support!) and would have thus made the lesson we wished to teach him harder to absorb. Pippa needed HIS FULL AND UNDIVIDED ATTENTION if she were to continue to persuade him, as she had already done so successfully in the stable, TO COME TO HER and allow her to put on his halter.

So the obliging Bronco was put out first in a little adjoining paddock: a calm, unobtrusive companion, just near enough to establish confidence in a newcomer, but well out of reach of argumentative teeth and heels. And sure enough the very first thing that Peter's sharp eyes spotted, as Pippa led him out into his new field, was Bronco's comforting if somewhat impolite back view! For Bronco did not consider it necessary to turn round and welcome this tiresome interloper. He had other and more important business on hand in confining his full attention to his own grazing. But there he was, a safe anchorage, and Peter would have no wish to wander far from his reassuring, if unfriendly, presence.

How carefully Pippa led Peter out of his stable and up to his new field, having first of all taken the wise precaution of visiting him once or twice beforehand, REPEATING yet again, IN HIS STABLE, the lesson with the halter they had practised so many times together the day before. So THIS LESSON WAS VERY FRESH IN PETER'S MIND as Pippa led him out.

Once more, Pippa's movements were EXAGGERATEDLY quiet and gentle as she led him, and with a finger resting lightly on the noseband of his head collar, she scratched his cheek comfortingly and spoke to him quietly as she led him along.

(We took the necessary precaution of putting on a head collar, for as most of us know, to turn out a horse into a strange field—even though he may APPEAR to be easy to catch—with nothing on his head, is simply asking for trouble until he really feels at home and begins to KNOW HIS NEW OWNERS.)

(You can read about this at greater length in *Your Book on Keeping Ponies*.)

When they reached the paddock, Pippa DID NOT let Peter go free at once. Instead, she stood by him, holding the end of the halter rope lightly, talking to him quietly, picking handfuls of grass and handing them to him, trying to explain to him AS BEST SHE COULD BY HER ACTIONS (the ONLY WAY we can really communicate satisfactorily with animals) that she too wished to share his pleasure at being outside again in the sunshine and fresh air and wanted to help and advise him as to which bits of grass he might find the most palatable!

Peter did not altogether approve of Pippa's choice in grass. He ignored her offerings and sniffed out better for himself. But he was pleasantly surprised at this unaccustomed turn of events. He associated being put out into a field with noise, clatter, a halter snatched off, a hearty wallop on the rump and . . . 'Off for the summer my lad!' and away he went. Whereas here—in this strangest of new homes—here was this quiet and inoffensive little owner actually staying out in the field with him helping to sample and choose each mouthful he ate! And there over the fence was that solid

Bronco, calm, unruffled and apparently entirely unmoved by any sight or sound. As he gazed round, his sharp old eye took in at a glance the cramped dimensions of this tiny paddock. This was surely no field in which to spend the whole summer. To Peter it looked little larger than an open-air stable.

And this is exactly what we had intended this little paddock to be. An open-air stable, where Pippa could continue her lessons of yesterday, in surroundings so confined that there would be no incentive whatsoever to gallop.

Before Pippa slipped off his halter to leave him, she gave him a titbit, and as Peter stood there chewing it, AND BEFORE HE HAD SO MUCH AS SWALLOWED IT, she held out the now familiar halter and once again asked Peter to drop his nose into it. Almost automatically now, and giving the matter little thought, Peter did as he was asked. Pippa slipped the halter VERY CARE-FULLY over his head once more and then quickly rewarded him with his usual titbit. Then slipping off the halter again, AS GENTLY and QUIETLY as she had put it on, she turned her back and walked away.

Peter was again taken by surprise. A less pleasant surprise this time for he was beginning to rather like his new little friend with her titbits. He actually wished she had stayed with him longer AND THIS IS JUST HOW WE HOPED HE WOULD FEEL.

In half an hour or so Pippa visited him again (just exactly as she had paid him repeated visits the day before in the stable). Just as before, she went quietly and slowly towards him and then, standing still and holding out the halter, she called his name. To HER surprise, and to her great delight, Peter this time came across the little field to her without hesitation and dropping his nose into the halter, just as he had done so many times the day before in the stable, he allowed her to put it over his head as he patiently waited for his reward.

Well done, Pippa. Peter's first lesson was all but learnt.

But let us not congratulate ourselves too soon for things might not run quite so smoothly when we turned Peter out into a big field. However, before we ventured to do so there was still something else Peter must learn while still safely confined in his present tiny paddock.

So far he had learned to come to Pippa and allow himself to be haltered whenever she cared to visit him, and when evening came and the sun had gone down, he was perfectly prepared to come in willingly enough, pangs of hunger having made a feed in his stable seem very desirable.

But would he be quite as ready and anxious to come again AT ANY TIME OF THE DAY—perhaps not long after he had been turned out—when Pippa wanted to ride him? If he were to be kept successfully on the Combined System this was another important lesson that must be quickly learnt and another which would be more easily taught while he was still confined in the small space of this tiny paddock.

Pippa thought this sounded very simple and one morning an hour or so after she had turned him out, she went back full of confidence to fetch him in again.

As usual he came to her at once when she called him and stood, lamb-like, while she put on his halter. But when she attempted to lead him back to the gate, to her surprise and alarm he threw up his head with an indignant snort, and digging his large toes firmly into the ground he made it quite clear that nothing would induce him to budge. With ears laid back and rolling eye he indicated that if Pippa attempted to drag him back into that stuffy old stable when he had just come out, she must be prepared to reap unpleasant consequences.

Pippa was taken aback. This was the first time she had witnessed Peter in such a mood. The Huntsman's dire warnings rang in her ears. 'You mind now . . . that old horse can be an awkward customer at times . . .' he had hinted darkly.

For a minute Pippa wondered what to do. But fortunately we had already tried to impress upon her a useful piece of advice. When a horse throws up his head NEVER TRY TO HOLD IT DOWN AGAIN BY FORCE it only becomes a losing battle with the odds heavily loaded to the stronger sparring partner —the horse. No horse really wishes to go about with his head in the air. Neither does he really enjoy walking backwards, bumping into unseen hazards behind him. But as most of us already know, EVERY HORSE WILL FIGHT AGAINST FORCE. IF YOU PULL HIM, HE WILL PULL YOU. But it takes two teams to make a tug-of-war. If one team stops pulling the contest inevitably collapses!

So when a horse throws up his head, IF NO RESISTANCE IS OFFERED, he very soon puts it down again.

Fortunately Pippa remembered this piece of advice in the nick of time and she let her fingers slip quickly to the end of the halter rope and Peter, who was all prepared for the usual battle, found himself strangely baffled when no strength was applied and down came his head again while he paused for a minute to think out different tactics!

Pippa lost not a second of this moment of truce to win the next round and slipping her fingers into his noseband she scratched his cheek encouragingly and laughed at him gently. What a silly old boy he was to make such a fuss when all she wanted him to do was come in for a moment to sample something nice she had waiting for him; and although Peter did not, unfortunately, entirely understand her words—neither was he paying particular attention to them—he sensed the gist of her intentions, and as she tempted him along with the offer of a tasty titbit, AND AS SHE SEEMED IN NO PARTICULAR HURRY TO FORCE HIM INTO DOING ANYTHING SPECIAL, he felt very much inclined to follow her without further fuss.

She led him to his stable and there another surprise awaited him, a nice little bowl of oats; and what was even more unusual, Pippa stood beside him while he ate them and as soon as he had swallowed the last one she turned him round and led him out to his little paddock again!

'Well, I'll be blowed—how peculiar!' one could see Peter musing as he ambled over to the fence to make sure that Bronco had not been similarly spirited away.

Bronco was still there. No one had seen fit to bring HIM indoors for an extra feed and he saw no reason why it was necessary for others to be so indulged. He left no doubt as to his disapproval by turning his back upon Peter and walking right away!

During the next few days Pippa, THROUGH CONSTANT REPETITION, made quite sure that Peter had learnt and absorbed this second lesson—to come into the stable willingly and amiably at any time of the day—whenever in fact he might be needed. And Peter soon accepted this unusual arrangement of being fetched in at odd times for odd meals as yet another of the strange idiosyncrasies of his new home!

Whilst Pippa had been thus engaged in teaching Peter she had herself learnt two useful lessons. First—never to offer resistance when a horse suddenly throws up his head: a lesson she was going to remember and find very useful later when riding Peter. And second—if a horse is kept successfully on the Combined System, when he will have to get used to being brought in at varying times during his 'grazing' hours for work (sometimes possibly very soon after he has been turned out) HE MUST BE CERTAIN OF ALWAYS FINDING A REWARD WAITING FOR HIM in the shape of a tasty feed. To bring him in to an EMPTY STABLE, only to throw on the saddle and bridle and hustle him off to work, will sooner or later end in inevitable trouble, and it will not be long before he decides that it is much more enjoyable staying out in the field, and he will soon think out very tiresome but extremely effective ways of evading capture!

So at last the day arrived when these first lessons were nearly complete. There was just one final step to take. We had to turn Peter out into a large field and see if, away from the safe confines of his tiny paddock, he would still allow himself to be haltered and caught.

Pippa embarked upon this with some trepidation for when Peter found himself with several wide acres in which to roam would he ever come to her? But to her suprise and great delight, he did!

With the greatest care and forgetting NO DETAILS, she repeated EXACTLY everything she had done when she first put him out into the small field:

1. She took him out quietly and INSTEAD OF IMMEDIATELY LETTING HIM GO, she stayed with him, watching him graze.
2. She led him about to get used to his new surroundings.
3. She offered him samples of grass and made it as plain as she could that SHE TOO wanted to share his pleasure in his new-found fortune.
4. And when she felt he had quite settled down and fully understood, she slipped off his halter, ONLY TO ASK HIM QUIETLY TO PUT IT ON AGAIN a minute later.

27

Peter remembered it all and when Pippa visited him again very frequently that first day in his large new paddock, he came to her willingly enough and allowed himself to be haltered IN EXCHANGE FOR HIS REWARD!

As an extra precaution we had once again put the patient Bronco in a little paddock alongside the larger field—A SAFE ANCHORAGE AGAIN, ALWAYS WITHIN SIGHT, YET NOT A 'GALLOPING COMPANION' IN THE SAME FIELD—and what a wise precaution it turned out to be! For alas, this happy state of affairs did not last long. All too soon there came the inevitable setback. One stormy day when the 'wind got under Peter's tail' and made him feel on edge and skittish, he decided to choose this inopportune moment to have an extra good roll and off came his head collar!

When Pippa went out to fetch him in her heart sank considerably lower than her boots! She could see at a glance what sort of mood he was in; the roaring wind drowned her voice as she called him; and there, lying in the mud, lay that vital head collar. Certainly, so far she had never actually had to rely upon the head collar to catch Peter. But she had always had the satisfaction of feeling that it was there and it was a comforting thought that, in an emergency, she could slip a finger through the noseband while she lifted the halter over his head. But now on this stormy day—the very moment when it might well be needed—Peter had managed to shake it off.

Worse still, although Peter came towards her quite oblivious that he had lost his head collar and quite willing to come up as usual, as he drew nearer, AS ALWAYS HAPPENS WITH HORSES, PIPPA'S ANXIETY TRANSMITTED ITSELF TO HIM. He dropped his nose into the outstretched halter as usual but he felt jumpy and suspicious and Pippa, in a vain endeavour to get that halter over his head today at any cost, bungled things badly. Gone were those quiet, gentle movements and instead of lifting the halter carefully right over his ears, she hurried, fumbled carelessly and roughly in her haste.

AN ASSOCIATION OF IDEAS sped through Peter's mind (and this is JUST HOW HORSES THINK AND REACT). Vivid memories were revived of other moments of 'capture': frantic efforts made to grab him; halters and ropes thrown at him; noise; discord; rounding up; and every trick of the trade.

28

He knew it all and was an artist at evasion. Up went his head and with a snort of derision he was soon rid of that halter—as he had flung off many a one before—and the wind, as though to punish him, blew the end of the rope against his neck, and gave him a smack. Without pausing to think he was quick to retaliate and whipping round on Pippa he lashed out at her with his large and formidable heels, as he had lashed out at many unsuccessful 'captors' before her. And out of the corner of his eye, as he galloped away, he had the satisfaction of noticing that she had jumped very nervously out of the way!

Pippa, as she stood and watched him go, saw a new friendship, so patiently and laboriously forged, shattered to smithereens in a few seconds. And what was even more disturbing, for the first time she began to feel a little frightened of Peter. She turned and left him and when she reached the house she was nearly in tears. But we tentatively suggested a new line of approach and Pippa, taking fresh heart, pluckily went out to try again.

But this time she made her way to Bronco's little field. He was delighted to see her! He had already had quite enough of playing 'anchor' to Peter and saw no reason why he should be expected to stay out any longer in this unpleasant wind. So when he saw Pippa coming he hailed her loudly, calling and nickering with the greatest pleasure; and Peter, who was as usual not very far off, pricked up his ears and wondered what could be the cause of Bronco's enthusiastic welcome. What could have inspired stodgy old Bronco to let off sounds of such tumultuous delight? And there, somewhat to his surprise, he saw Pippa INSIDE Bronco's little field apparently making a great fuss of him and feeding him large quantities of tasty titbits!

Bronco could hardly believe in his new-found good luck and he continued to ask loudly and greedily for more and more!

Although Peter was certainly not going to give the game away by allowing anyone to imagine for one moment that he was in the LEAST BIT INTERESTED, nevertheless as he grazed he kept a very sharp eye upon the proceedings. Nearer and nearer he came and though never lifting his head and to all intents and purposes entirely engrossed in grass, gradually, step by step, he worked his way right up to Bronco's fence.

And Pippa, who was INSIDE Bronco's field—with that fence between them as a safe protection from Peter's heels—felt full confidence again.

ONCE MORE PIPPA'S FEELINGS SOON TRAVELLED ACROSS THAT IN-EXPLICABLE, INVISIBLE WAVE TO PETER, and HER confidence, happily restored, quickly transmitted itself to him.

'Not frightened of me any more!' he mused as he went on grazing near Pippa and Bronco, and in the depths of his heart Peter felt VERY relieved. For nothing is so disturbing and upsetting to a horse—or for that matter to any animal—than nervousness on the part of humans. It arouses immediate suspicion, destroys at once any hope of co-operation and obedience, and puts the animal on the defensive; moreover, it leaves him feeling suddenly lost and rather bewildered like an army whose officers have all fled. Few of us can avoid at times feeling frightened if we have to try to handle difficult and strange animals, but by dint of a little ingenuity, some means can usually be found of preventing them from realizing it!

So Pippa, by this simple ruse of standing behind Bronco's fence, not only FELT safer, but WAS safely out of reach of Peter's heels and so self-confidence soon became restored again all round.

The next step was easy. Pippa simply played a little game with Peter over that fence. First she continued to give Bronco titbits, and very soon pangs of green-eyed jealousy began to stir in Peter's contrite heart! In next to no time he was leaning over the fence nudging her for his share.

'Yes, you shall have something,' Pippa told him, 'but ONLY if you are a good boy and put your nose into a halter first!' And Pippa held out to him, OVER THE FENCE, an old halter with the lead rope cut off which we had advised her to take along in her pocket as extra ammunition with the titbits!

(You can read about the usefulness of these old cut-down halters and the helpful part they can play in just such a situation, in *Your Book on Keeping Ponies*.)

To have attempted to put on Peter's head collar OVER THE FENCE might well have led to further trouble. A head collar is comparatively large and heavy and needs a certain amount of adjusting. A false move would have sent Peter flying off again, certainly never to return a second time!

30

So instead, Pippa held out this old halter and by dint of a little patient coaxing and a few laughs and jokes as she played the little game of first trying it on Bronco and then persuading Peter to 'have a go', good humour was soon restored and the old halter safely and securely fastened on Peter's head. Then wisely Pippa turned her back upon Peter and continued her ardent attentions to Bronco! Peter walked away in a huff. But as he felt quite free, and as Pippa APPEARED TO BE IN NO PARTICULAR HASTE TO BOTHER WITH HIM FURTHER, all those unhappy thoughts and associations of recent misunderstandings and mismanagement soon began to fade away and when Pippa ventured out from behind Bronco's fence and called him to her, Peter came willingly enough and allowed himself to be haltered as though nothing had happened.

The hatchet was safely buried.

But Pippa was going to look back later upon this little episode as further useful experience gained. For that windy day was the first, but not the last, occasion on which Peter's feelings were ruffled so that his heels were presented in unpleasant evidence again.

There came the day later on when the vet arrived to attend to Peter's teeth and Pippa was not available to fetch him in. But the vet, who had seen him coming up before so quickly and obediently when Pippa called him, thought he was 'foolproof to catch' and off he went to the field, laughing and chatting to his assistant. They did not get very near Peter! And his aggressive attitude puzzled and rather annoyed them for they were busy men and had little time to waste. Pippa too was puzzled when she went later to fetch Peter in and to her surprise he behaved in exactly the same way as he had on that fateful windy day. He threw up his head with a snort and shook it free of his halter, just as she was about to put it on, whipping round on her, pretending to kick out, although she noticed that this time his aim was NOT very accurate nor his intentions too serious. But he was telling her as plainly as he could that he had temporarily lost faith again. She had let him down by sending strange men to 'round him up' and he would have none of her.

So once more she had to devote an afternoon to re-establishing confidence and good humour by dint of the same little ruse from behind Bronco's fence, and by playing the same little game again.

Then there was yet another occasion when a school friend wanted to try catching Peter and bringing him in. But despite careful instructions from Pippa as to EXACTLY how to proceed, the details, alas, only went in through one young ear to escape quickly from the other! For had not this young friend ridden all her life and had several ponies of her own? Why all this fuss and bother when catching Peter? She would show Pippa a thing or two! And somehow, thanks to Peter's careful training, she did just manage to get his halter on before he thought of turning tail and flying from this tempestuous and speedy stranger. But he stored up careful memory of her unpleasant, rough little hands and the way she snatched at his mane and grabbed him. He mused about it all night long, and when Pippa went to fetch him next day he vented his wrath and indignation upon HER again. Just the same snorts as she tried to halter him; just the same show of heels before he whisked round and galloped away; and Pippa had to resort once more to all the same old tactics and devote a long time again to restoring order, obedience and confidence, and to patching up their precious friendship.

But once again it was Pippa, as well as Peter, who had absorbed and realized, through the light of bitter experience, two more valuable truths.

One was that when teaching or training a horse, even in the most simple matter, if things go wrong—IF HE FAILS TO UNDERSTAND—in fact, if any setback occurs, one MUST revert to the first lessons again, starting if necessary RIGHT FROM THE BEGINNING ONCE MORE. It may seem disheartening; it will certainly be tedious; but in the end it is the quickest way, FOR NO REAL PROGRESS CAN OTHERWISE BE MADE.

The other point that struck Pippa, after her school friend's clumsy attempts to capture Peter, was that it was UNWISE AT PRESENT TO LET OTHER PEOPLE HANDLE HIM AT ALL UNLESS THEY WERE PREPARED TO CARRY OUT HER INSTRUCTIONS TO THE LETTER. 'In fact I think I see now,' she said, 'why people with well-schooled horses do not care about letting

David Tamplin

Before trying to teach your horse to come when he is called, begin by learning to hold the halter correctly.

Like this:

With the slack end neatly folded across the palm of the hand.

NOT LIKE THIS—

With the slack end hanging down, which can be dangerous and can easily frighten the horse.
(Remember, once he has been frightened, the lesson takes MUCH longer to learn.)

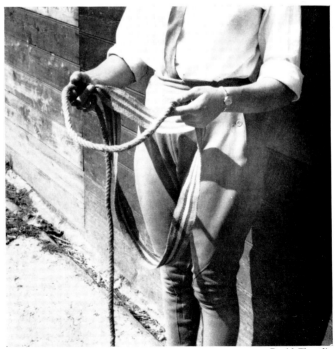

David Tamplin

Start the lesson in an enclosed yard; small, confined paddock, or even in the stable itself. Approach the horse DIRECTLY in front of his head, holding out the halter exactly as shown in the previous picture, and encourage HIM TO STEP TOWARDS YOU and to DROP HIS NOSE into your outstretched halter loop.

AS SOON AS HE HAS DONE SO (but NOT before) reward him IMMEDIATELY with a titbit.

Once he will come to you—even if only a few steps—and drop his nose quietly and confidently into the halter loop, you may congratulate yourself that the battle is all but won!

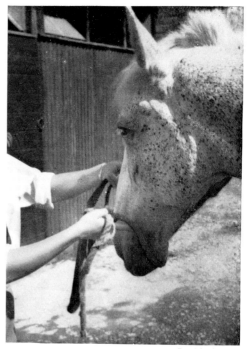

David Tamplin

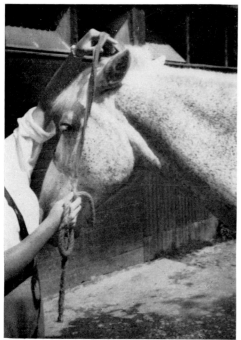

David Tamplin

The next step is to slip the halter right over his head, but be sure not to ABUSE HIS CONFIDENCE by doing this roughly or hastily.

Instead, raise the halter slowly and gently with a protecting hand slipped under the head piece like this . . .

Making doubly sure not to drag it carelessly over his ears.

(Remember, some horses are very sensitive about the ears. Especially so if they have been at some time subjected to the twitch.)

David Tamplin

Lastly, hold the slack end of the rope gently but firmly with your LEFT hand—just as you see here,

David Tamplin

while you make the knot.

NEVER FORGET THE KNOT,

for if left unknotted, the rope will pull taut and either frighten or hurt the horse, making him VERY loath to come to you again, much less risk dropping his nose into the offending halter!

Or worse still, if left unknotted the whole thing will drop off and away he will go, never to be recaptured if he can possibly avoid it!

Peter arrived with the reputation of being a rare old rascal, impossible to catch once he had been turned out in a field!

But by following these instructions to the letter, Pippa soon managed to teach him to come to her when he was called.

But having done so, Pippa NEVER dragged him straight in from the field.

David Tamplin

Instead, she always stood with him for a few minutes first; talking to him quietly; renewing and cementing their friendship.

To rush a horse straight in as soon as he is haltered savours too much of 'capture'.

Pause awhile; chat to him; give him his titbits; and he will be only too delighted and willing to come again next time he is called.

their friends ride them, because it might mean re-schooling them all over again afterwards!'

Well done, Pippa, she had certainly stumbled across something worth remembering for, as she could plainly see for herself, a horse's good manners, obedience and even his CONFIDENCE IN HIS OWNER can in a very short space of time be ruined by someone either less experienced, or someone who neither UNDERSTANDS NOR IS PREPARED TO FOLLOW THE SAME PATTERN AND RULE OF HANDLING OR RIDING HIM.

'And what a long time such teaching takes,' sighed Pippa as she looked back upon the hours, mounting to days and even weeks, that we had spent in getting Peter accustomed to his new routine of living under the Combined System where he would benefit from all the comforts of stable life, but at the same time enjoy daily the freedom of the fields. But if this system was to run smoothly Peter must learn to forsake the pleasures of leisure and freedom and COME UP when called and COME IN WILLINGLY whenever needed.

What a long time it had taken to teach him such simple lessons, and what a long chapter this is, and how many words have been needed to explain such an elementary procedure in such detail! But if a settled, humdrum routine, A GENTLE SOWING OF THE SEEDS OF DISCIPLINE, AND A DAWNING CONFIDENCE AND REAL FRIENDSHIP WITH HIS OWNER FIRST BE ESTABLISHED, THE TRAINING OR RE-TRAINING OF ANY ANIMAL BECOMES VERY MUCH EASIER LATER ON.

As the old masters of the true art of equitation are continually reminding us . . . '*Calme Avant Droit*' is the goal at which to aim. The first ingredient of this recipe is calm and tranquillity. And AT HOME, in field and stable, is the best place to start encouraging and cultivating this 'Peace of Mind'.

YOUR LESSON

TEACHING YOUR HORSE TO COME UP WHEN HE IS CALLED

The first step towards improving your riding is to teach and encourage better manners in your horse AT HOME, IN FIELD *and* IN STABLE. *Yours and his more advanced lessons must progress hand in hand together, and you will soon find that if your horse is to be expected to give you his full attention he must begin each lesson in a* CALM *and* TRANQUIL *frame of mind.*

To be obliged to chase after him round his field, for instance, and to capture him by means of 'wild-west tactics' before the ride starts, will NOT *improve his powers of concentration nor enhance a spirit of co-operation and obedience.*

Also, if he is to be kept on the Combined System—that is, living in the stable at night and running out in the fields for fresh air and exercise during the day (usually the best method of keeping a horse that is being schooled or re-schooled), he must, of necessity, be ready to come in from that field willingly, whenever he is wanted, otherwise there can be no ride at all!

Teach him, therefore, from the beginning, to come to you when he is called.

A little patience; some perseverance; THE CORRECT TACTICS; *and the most erring sinner can soon be taught.*

Start the lesson in an enclosed yard; a small confined paddock; or even in the loose box itself.

Approach the horse DIRECTLY IN FRONT, *holding out the halter exactly as shown in the photographs, and encourage* HIM *to* STEP TOWARDS YOU (*even though to begin with it may only be half a step at a time!*). *Then very quietly, and by dint of a little*

34

gentle persuasion and the tempting sight of a titbit or two poking out of your pocket, try to get him to DROP HIS NOSE INTO THAT OUTSTRETCHED LOOP.

The moment he has actually dropped his nose into the loop—BUT NOT BEFORE—*reward him at once with the titbit.*

So much for the first round. This is quite enough to begin with. Go right away and leave him alone. But return later, at suitably spaced intervals throughout the day, and repeat the lesson UNTIL HE WILL COME UP TO YOU WILLINGLY *and* DROP HIS NOSE INTO THE HALTER *loop in order to get that titbit! When he will do this without hesitation,* THEN—*but not before*—*begin gently putting the halter right on, rewarding him once more when it is finally in place.*

After a continual repetition of this lesson in an enclosed place, you will find it will not be long before you can turn him out into a large field and he will still come to you willingly and obediently when he is wanted.

ABOUT PIPPA AND PETER

2 · *Mounting Lightly*

This chapter is going to be just as short as the last one was long, for very few words will be needed to describe how Pippa herself caused the next backward step in our programme.

We decided one day that the time had at last arrived to start riding Peter. Pippa could hardly wait to begin, although she did curb her impatience to the extent of taking all the usual pains and precautions while getting Peter ready for this great event.

(Point One) How carefully and quietly she called him up from the far end of the field.

(Point Two) How patiently she waited while he digested his titbit and they had a little 'chat' together.

(Point Three) How slowly they dawdled along to the stable, with Pippa's fingers—which by now had become 'feather-light'—just guiding him, as she slipped them as usual through his nose band. (Look at the photograph.)

(Point Four) How quiet and methodical was the grooming. Indeed, Peter hardly noticed what was going on, so busy was he enjoying the tasty feed that, as usual, he had found waiting in his stable for him.

(Point Five) And so gently did the saddle descend upon his back that, unaccustomed as he was to the feel of it after so many idle weeks, he took no umbrage at the thought of work again!

Indeed he walked out into the yard when bidden, so dozily, so quiet, so

36

RELAXED and in such a tranquil frame of mind that he immediately settled himself comfortably in the sunshine, one hind leg resting, eyes half closed, all ready and prepared to take a little nap while awaiting further pleasant developments.

So far so good, Pippa had managed splendidly and had brought Peter out saddled and bridled, IN JUST THE RIGHT, CALM FRAME OF MIND THAT WOULD BE NEEDED IF WE WERE TO CAPTURE HIS FULL POWERS OF CONCENTRATION and take his re-education one step further.

But alas, our congratulations proved to be a little premature. For things did not continue to run quite so smoothly. As soon as Pippa was ready to mount, that Jovial Huntsman's words rang suddenly in her ears again. 'You look sharp, young lady, when you get up the first time,' he had warned. 'For that old horse can't bear to be kept standing around. You'll find you have to jump up into the saddle pretty slick, at double quick time, if you want to get there at all!' He had laughed.

Pippa must certainly have decided to take him at his word for before one could say 'Jack Robinson' she had snatched up the reins and somehow or another scrambled aboard, giving poor Peter a good dig in the ribs with her toe and a hearty kick on the quarters with her foot as she wriggled and struggled into the saddle.

Poor Peter! What a rude awakening from his comfortable apathy. Indeed, HIS WHOLE MOOD OF HAPPY, CONFIDENT, TRANQUILLITY that Pippa had taken such pains to create—not only on this particular morning but during all these past weeks—this happy, quiet mood was shattered, just like a pane of glass through which someone has thrown a brick.

With a snort of alarm and astonishment he threw up his head and hit Pippa sharply on the nose (for we had omitted to carry out the Huntsman's instructions and strap down his head with a tight-standing martingale!) and then he proceeded backwards at some speed straight into a couple of stable buckets. What a clatter! Pippa instinctively gave him a good kick in the ribs to disentangle him from the buckets and at this fresh insult he shot forward again and would have been off, full speed down the drive, had not the yard gate fortunately been firmly shut!

37

Mounting Lightly

We suggested that the wisest thing under the circumstances would be for Pippa to dismount again, which she was already in the process of doing, even more swiftly than she had got up, giving the unfortunate Peter a few more kicks over the quarters as she slithered hastily to the safety of *terra firma*!

What a grave mistake poor Pippa had made, for she could now see plainly for herself that there is little object in spending endless time and devoting much patience to cultivating in a horse a happy, calm, tranquil and CONFI-DENT frame of mind, NOR IS THERE MUCH HOPE OF EXPECTING HIM TO REMAIN IN A TRANQUIL MOOD WHILE BEING RIDDEN, IF ONE STARTS THE RIDE IN SUCH A CLUMSY AND UNCOMFORTABLE FASHION. Good humour and confidence are bound to be quickly dispelled by a hasty, painful and tempestuous scramble on to a horse's back, punctuated by a kick in the ribs, a bang on the quarters, and as a final touch, with saddle pulled uncomfortably awry.

If this was the type of assault Peter had constantly been led to expect, small wonder that he had aquired a reputation of backing, fidgeting, crab-walking, refusing to stand still, and being thoroughly difficult to mount.

Pippa was inclined to agree that one could hardly blame him; and, what was even more important, she was beginning to realize that there could only be one cure. If we wished to teach him to mend his ways and to stand quietly and patiently while his rider mounted, there was only ONE WAY to set about it, and that was TO MAKE IT INTERESTING AND COMFORTABLE FOR HIM TO DO SO (just exactly as we had made it pleasant and interesting for him, by dint of patience and 'titbits', to come from the farthest corner of the field whenever he was called).

This time, however, we must put first things first and realize that before hoping to teach a horse to stand still to be mounted THE RIDER HIMSELF MUST FIRST PRACTISE LANDING LIGHTLY IN THE SADDLE. So before we attempted to re-educate Peter on this point we suggested that it was Pippa who must first learn the new lesson by practising the gentle art of springing —not on to poor Peter, but on to a stout stone wall!

(Look at the photos and you will see how we set about this.)

In another book entitled *Learning to Ride* by the same author, and issued by the same publisher, you can see another small girl being given a 'leg up' during her first riding lessons, so that FROM THE START she may learn to land lightly in the saddle.

Although Pippa had been riding for several years no one as yet had apparently suggested this idea to her. So she had been cheerfully and unconsciously digging her toe into innumerable horses' sides and scrambling up clumsily into countless saddles, quite oblivious of the discomfort she had been causing!

So this time it was Pippa who had to take herself in hand first, by spending several days in having a 'leg up' until she could land like a feather on the 'saddle' on the wall!

While she was thus engrossed, Peter returned thankfully to his pleasant routine of browsing round his broad acres, and so peaceful and happy were his days that he soon forgot all about his young mistress's precipitous and tumultuous assault on to his back. This time he took no umbrage at her mistakes but continued to come cheerfully and obediently to her when she came to call him; and as she led him in from the field she whispered repeatedly into his ear that her undignified scramble on to his back had been a big mistake and would never, never happen again! Peter evidently believed her for to Pippa's everlasting surprise and astonishment the next time she attempted to mount him he STOOD QUITE STILL.

But perhaps in all fairness to the reader we should add that this miracle was not entirely due to Pippa's efforts, but partly to the fact that we took the extra precaution of having another helper standing in front of Peter offering him a tasty titbit to divert his thoughts and prevent a fit of the fidgets; and by constant repetition of this simple little ruse for a few days Peter soon forgot his old tiresome habits and learnt to stand rock still until his rider gave him the signal to move off.

So can any horse, however erring in his ways, be taught in a very short space of time to stand quietly to be mounted if these simple instructions are carried out.

Perhaps you may know of a fidgety horse in need of such timely correction? If you do, try out these simple experiments for yourself. But before you embark upon his lesson just turn back for a minute to the beginning of this chapter and make quite certain you leave no small stone unturned. Refresh your memory upon each point to consider:

1. Lead up to the lesson by the QUIET, UNHURRIED saddling and bridling in the stable, so that when the horse is brought out HE IS IN SUITABLE, CALM and TRANQUIL FRAME OF MIND in which he will be agreeable and able to pay FULL ATTENTION to what he is supposed to be doing.

2. MAKE CERTAIN that the rider has himself first practised and learnt his share of the lesson by being able to land LIGHTLY and EXPERTLY in the saddle—and having landed is PREPARED TO SIT STILL.

3. Have someone ready to give the rider a 'leg up', someone who is used to doing so and will lift him up swiftly and without hesitation or argument.

4. And lastly have another helper standing fair and square right in front of the horse ready to reward him instantly with a little titbit if he stands quietly, sedately and patiently.

Then if these simple instructions are faithfully carried out you may be almost certain of success. But remember once again that (as usual) it is the rider himself who must make the real effort by first practising the gentle art of LANDING LIGHTLY.

Before attempting to teach your horse to stand still to be mounted, once again FIRST TAKE YOURSELF IN HAND and make sure that YOU can mount swiftly, quietly and expertly and, above all, will land like a FEATHER in the saddle.

Pippa practises with an old felt saddle balanced precariously on a stout stone wall. . . .

. . . first a 'leg up' . . .

. . . then she tries springing up alone and landing LIGHTLY.

(The saddle soon comes adrift if she is clumsy!)

When Peter first came he strongly objected to being asked to stand still to be mounted and, as you will read in the story, Pippa's clumsy attempts to scramble on to his back did not exactly help matters!

But having practised on the wall (just as you can see her doing in the picture) and HERSELF BECOME MORE EXPERT . . .

David Tamplin

. . . Pippa asked a friend to give her a 'leg up' (lest she inadvertently dig her toe into Peter's side and upset him again), whilst another helper stood directly in front of him ready to reward him handsomely with a titbit if he DID manage to keep still! . . .

David Tamplin

. . . and it all worked like a charm!

(You try this simple lesson if your horse too is a fidget. But remember, as usual, it is the RIDER who must be tackled FIRST!)

YOUR LESSON

Teaching Your Horse To Stand Still To Be Mounted

As you will read in the story, Pippa's first attempt at scrambling on to Peter's back was so rough and amateurish that he objected very strongly indeed and needless to say he refused to stand still! And it did not take long to dawn upon Pippa that it was SHE *who must first learn to mount more expertly before she attempted to improve Peter's manners.*

Are you sure that your efforts at mounting leave no room for improvement? For one can hardly expect any horse to give his full attention to standing still to be mounted if his rider flops on to his back like a sack of potatoes, giving him a good dig in the ribs and kick on the quarters in passing. Not to mention probably pulling the saddle awry at the same time!

So before you attempt to teach your horse to stand still, take yourself in hand and really learn to mount lightly and expertly, landing like a veritable FEATHER *in the saddle.*

A garden wall makes an excellent 'hobby-horse' for all these exercises and experiments: or failing a wall, an empty cider barrel propped up to a suitable height by adding some legs is just as good; or you may be lucky enough to acquire a second-hand gymnasium 'horse'.

Start the practice by getting someone to give you a 'leg-up' and see how LIGHTLY *you can jump and how* GENTLY *you can land. Then try springing alone.*

To make matters a little more difficult, try lodging a child's felt pony saddle, or just a felt numdah on your 'hobby-horse'. It will soon come unstuck if your efforts are still clumsy!

Mounting Lightly

*When you really feel you have become rather an expert—*BUT NOT BEFORE—*then begin thinking about teaching your horse to stand still, by the very simple means of getting someone to give you a 'leg-up' (lest you might still be tempted to dig your toe into his side) while another helper, standing directly in front of him, rewards the horse with a nice titbit* IF *and* WHEN *he behaves well and does not move.*

By this means, the most fidgety sinner can very soon be taught to stand like a rock to be mounted.

But remember once more that it is the RIDER *who must first learn to* LAND LIGHTLY *in the saddle. For no horse can be expected to stand stock still if he is very uncomfortable. Would you?*

ABOUT PIPPA AND PETER

3 · *Sitting in Better Position*

And now we must hurry along, for although Peter had stood still to be mounted—thanks to his new lesson and his rider's ability to land lightly in the saddle—one cannot keep him standing forever. Indeed the old adage should always be borne in mind—NEVER KEEP A FIT HORSE WAITING. Bring him out of the stable quietly, mount LIGHTLY, SWIFTLY and EXPERTLY, and then MOVE OFF, with no dawdling or gossiping. Then the horse will be ready and keen to do what is asked of him to the best of his ability.

So rather than keep Peter hanging about one minute longer than necessary in the yard, we suggested that Pippa try him out round the circular drive in front of the house.

But oh dear! When we noticed, before they left the yard, how Pippa was sitting our heart sank a little (have a good look at the picture and see if you can spot anything wrong).

As soon as the yard gate was opened and Peter moved quickly forward anxious to be off, as we had foreseen, Pippa, taken unawares, lurched back in the saddle giving the unfortunate Peter the INEVITABLE jab in the mouth as she did so. Although the jab was only a slight one it was quite enough to disconcert Peter almost as much as Pippa's first attempts at mounting had done and his reactions were not dissimilar.

Up went his head, coming again in swift and painful contact with poor

43

Pippa's nose. 'Had we not better do as the Huntsman suggested and put on a standing martingale? Anyway, just until I get used to him?' Pippa asked tentatively as she rubbed her tender nose. But before we had time to explain that no number of martingales—however tightly they may be strapped down—would cure a fault in the rider, they were off again at rather a swifter pace than Pippa had bargained for until, confronted by the corner of the drive that led home to the stables, Peter dug in his toes and refused to move at all!

Now what was to be done? Pippa gave him a good prod with her heels, and as this did not answer she was obliged (as you can see in the picture), to screw herself round in the saddle in order to give him a better kick in the ribs!

By now Peter's feelings were thoroughly ruffled and his patience nearly lost, as he indicated very clearly by swishing his tail (as you can see also in the photograph). Then off he set again at far too swift a walk, making Pippa feel—although she was loath to admit it—as though she had VERY little control! And when she did manage to stop him by dint of tugging and hauling the reins, DOWN went Peter's head this time, as he in his turn snatched and 'bored'. (Just look again and you can see him doing it!)

What could be wrong?

Perhaps you can guess? Take another good look at the way in which Pippa is sitting and perhaps you too will be able to see that once again the FAULT LAY WITH THE RIDER.

So for the second time it was Pippa's failings that had first to be tackled, then—as we hoped she herself would soon discover—Peter's shortcomings would miraculously melt away.

If you examine the pictures carefully you will notice that Pippa is sitting right on the back of her saddle (perhaps you yourself do the same?), the reason being that her stirrups are far too short and she is therefore pushed into this position. But it is on the back of the saddle, or near the 'cantle' as it is called, that one is bound to feel all the bumps and jolts. As the horse moves forward suddenly the rider cannot help but sway slightly backwards and AS HIS BODY LEANS BACK, SO BACK COME HIS HANDS at one and the same

44

time, and HE CANNOT AVOID GIVING THE HORSE A SLIGHT JAB IN THE MOUTH. Also, as you can plainly see, when the rider sitting like this wishes to move forward again, with his legs in this position, there is nothing he can do but give his horse a prod with his heels.

In fact sitting in this position offers only two alternatives—a kick in the ribs to 'go' and a haul at the reins to 'stop'! Simple expedients perhaps, but ones which rely largely upon brute force!

Pippa, therefore, sitting like this, could only attempt to control and master Peter by dint of strength alone and, as she herself was the first to admit, pitting her strength against Peter's was obviously doomed to failure from the word go!

But how else was she to be expected to manage him? Pippa questioned. There could be only one other way, and that was to find a method in which Pippa could EXPLAIN her wishes to him and ASK him to obey them in such a way that Peter would find it COMFORTABLE and INTERESTING to do so.

So just as we had found a method of making Peter

1. WISH TO COME TO PIPPA WHEN HE WAS CALLED

and

2. HAPPY TO STAND STOCK STILL WHILE SHE MOUNTED

we must now find a method of making obedience to her wishes when she is riding equally acceptable to him.

We must, in fact, try to control Peter and teach him to be controlled by the more gentle art of rather 'more advanced riding', and such riding CAN ONLY BE BUILT UPON THE FIRM FOUNDATION OF THE CORRECT POSITION OF THE RIDER IN THE SADDLE. For such riding demands that one 'SPEAKS' to the horse by means of simple 'SIGNS' and in course of time, WHEN HE FULLY UNDERSTANDS THEM, being at heart a gentle, peace-loving animal he will nearly always obey.

These signs have to be given chiefly with the LEGS; by the slight movement or deviation of the rider's WEIGHT in the saddle; and by HANDS that are so 'finger-light,' so QUIET, so STILL and so COMFORTABLE to the horse that never, in any circumstances, does the bit UPSET, HURT or disturb his tender mouth to the extent of upsetting his nerves and his feelings and rousing his

45

temper, or creating in him any feeling of opposition or anger, which would IMMEDIATELY promote in him a WISH TO CONTRADICT and do wrong.

But, as we have already seen, if the rider's hands are to remain STEADY and STILL so must his own position in the saddle also remain steady and still, regardless of the horse's sudden movements, and therefore it would seem that the obvious place for the rider to sit is where he is going to feel the fewest bumps and jolts.

As has already been mentioned, by sitting on the back of the saddle the rider gets bumps and jolts in full measure. For, as most of us already know, the greatest motion on a horse's back is spread over the region of his quarters and the least motion (or centre of gravity as it is sometimes called) is somewhere near the withers. Therefore the farther back we sit in the saddle the greater become the bumps, whereas the nearer we can PERCH over the WITHERS the less movement we are likely to feel.

How then to sit as near as possible to the horse's withers? With stirrups too short it just cannot be done!

1. The first step is to let down the leathers; then—
2. To press oneself down into the lowest part of the saddle.
3. To let our legs hang down over the girth.
4. To learn to sit in such a position that it will be easy to give signals to the horse through our legs and in which we can employ our weight to give further commands.
5. And lastly, to sit in a position where we will move as little as possible in the saddle—that is to say, where we move only by INTENT not by accident.

But as Pippa would quickly realize, to alter one's SEAT entirely requires a certain amount of practice; and rather than bore and irritate poor Peter with tiresome experiment, we suggested that Pippa should put him back in his stable again and return herself to the wall where once again exercises would be the order of the day!

You will see in the photographs how these exercises were carried out.

YOUR LESSON

LEARNING TO SIT IN A GOOD POSITION

Having mastered the art of mounting correctly, the next thing to think about is your position in the saddle.

We asked Pippa to jump up on the wall and show us just how she would sit on her horse.

Look at the picture and you will see how she sat—a nice round-backed-slouch, with knees cocked up and legs and feet all ready to slip into VERY *short stirrups!*

Now jump on to your 'hobby-horse' and take stock of yourself.

Perhaps you, too, sit in just this same fashion?

Sitting in this position there can only be one outcome—every time your horse moves suddenly you cannot help yourself but hang on by the reins. (Oh his poor mouth!) And when you want him to stop perhaps you brace those feet and give a good tug! With the unhappy result that the bit lodges on the corners of his mouth—or on the lips as it is sometimes called—just the VERY *place where he himself finds it easiest to pull back* VERY HARD *and generally with his mouth wide open!*

Just look again at the pictures.

And when you want him to go on again, with those short stirrups, there is little option but to give a good dig in the ribs with your heels to make him start.

It does not take much imagination to realize that 'kick-to-go', and 'pull-and-haul-to-stop' does not exactly constitute the art of equitation! But until the rider is sitting in a better position it is impossible to attempt any more advanced riding.

Sitting in Better Position

You will see in the story how Pippa was advised to alter her position by the very simple means of doing exercises on the wall. Look carefully at these exercises and try them out on your own 'hobby-horse'.

When you really feel you are beginning to improve, try again on a quiet horse as he moves along—if you can find one that is amiable and long-suffering enough to put up with it!—all the time keeping your goal in mind, which is to learn to sit in such a position that you can give commands and signals to your horse THROUGH YOUR LEGS *and the* WEIGHT OF YOUR BODY; *and where you yourself will move in the saddle* ONLY BY INTENT *and* NOT *by accident!*

Practice makes perfect. But it means long, hard and tedious practice if the muscles of your thighs and back are to become strong enough to KEEP *you in the correct position.*

Try hard. Do not be daunted. Stick to it.

FOR YOU WILL SOON SEE THAT THE CORRECT POSITION IN THE SADDLE IS THE FOUNDATION OF ALL MORE ADVANCED RIDING.

David Tamplin

We asked Pippa to jump up on the wall and show us just how she would sit on a horse.

Once astride the little felt saddle perched on the wall, this is exactly how she flopped into position!

Right on the back of the saddle; knees well cocked up, anticipating those VERY short stirrups; toes hanging down; and a nice, round back; all ready in a rest-ful, armchair-position in fact, to go bobbing along as a cheerful, but ineffectual, 'passenger'.

Have a good look at the photo and then take stock of yourself!

Perhaps you too sit in just this same fashion?

Richard Hammonds

Be honest with yourself! Be critical! Jump up on to YOUR wall or 'hobby-horse' and see if you too have a tendency to sit in this same position.

If you DO sit like this there can be but one outcome—every time your horse moves forward suddenly you cannot help but give him a jab in the mouth—be it ever so slight a one.

David Tamplin

Moreover, when you want him to stop perhaps you too brace those feet, lean back, and give an almighty tug!

Oh, his poor mouth! Not to mention your poor arms—for just look how the bit is lying on the corners of his mouth, the one place where he finds it easiest to pull hard too!

So however hard you may haul at the reins, ten to one he DOES NOT STOP!

To complete the experiment we let Pippa jump up and 'have a go' on Peter.

Once safely on board she looks very pleased with herself!

But when she tries to get him to move, he digs in his toes; refuses to budge; and swishes his tail with annoyance! However, undaunted, Pippa squirms round in the saddle and gives him a good kick in the ribs.

Highly indignant, Peter sets off rather faster than his rider bargained for!

Endeavouring to slow the pace, Pippa sticks her feet forwards and takes a good pull at the reins and down goes Peter's head as he tries to snatch them out of her hands!

One way and another, NOT a great success!
For sitting in this position makes more advanced riding (and the schooling of the horse) an impossibility.

Here are some exercises that helped Pippa to get into the right position.
You try them too!

David Tamplin

Stretch down those legs . .

David Tamplin

. . . as far as they will go!

David Tamplin

Try to keep those legs steady and in the same position . . .

David Tamplin

. . . while you do every exercise you can possibly invent.

David Tamplin

Instead of flopping into the saddle as you lounge in a chair, try sitting forwards; POISED; ready at all times to GO WITH YOUR HORSE as he himself is in constant, forward motion.

YOUR FEET

A vital factor; for if they are in the wrong position, everything else will go wrong too. So start at the bottom and work upwards!

Richard Hammonds

HEELS DOWN; TOES RAISED; with the ball of the foot and big toe joint (the spring-point of the body) ready to press on the stirrup iron and take your weight, as your whole body tends to SPRING—be it ever so slightly —forward . . . forward . . . at each step and movement of the horse.

AND YOUR ANKLES!

You will find it impossible to persuade those feet into this position if the ankles are stiff and bent the wrong way.

(Try, and see!)

So to encourage supple ankles first practise these exercises . . .

Richard Hammonds

dropping your toe

Richard Hammonds

. . . and waggling your foot round and round in either direction.

YOUR ELBOWS

Light hands stem from supple elbows. So here is an exercise that helps to make elbows softer and more pliable.

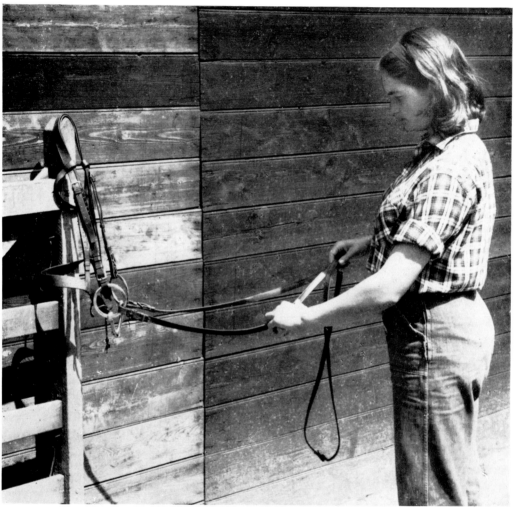

Hang up a bridle, back to front. Then stand up straight, with your shoulders back and see if you can manage to shorten the reins without permitting the dangling bit to move. When your elbows have become really supple you will find you can slide your fingers forwards down the reins so smoothly and gently that never a movement will there be from that bit in front of you.

But with stiff elbows HOW that bit will jangle!

Try it for yourself and see.

YOUR FINGERS

In more advanced riding a subtle 'squeeze' of the reins—the gentle pressure of individual fingers—is often enough to convey your thoughts and your wishes to a well-schooled horse.

So sitting in the correct and balanced position, get someone to hold the reins while you try exercising and manipulating those fingers.

Richard Hammonds

(You can see in the photo how gentle and sensitive those fingers are becoming.)

Yours could soon be just as good if you practise!

When you have satisfied yourself that you have carried out all these suggestions to the letter and feel that perfection has nearly been reached, then
borrow a quiet pony and with the help of a friend try these same exercises
mounted while the horse walks along.

Start each exercise with hands on hips. . . .

Richard Hammonds

. . . then hands on shoulders.

(Here you see Legend kindly offering his services and he happens to be just the chap for the job! Kind, quiet, long-suffering, very cheerful and only too anxious to oblige as long as he is not expected to exert HIMSELF at all!)

Richard Hammonds

With hands on the hips, try standing up in the stirrups, as the horse moves along and sitting down again SLOWLY and LIGHTLY.

(Not quite as easy as it looks! You try and see.)

Richard Hammonds

Then think about fingers again . . . hands on your hips . . . on your shoulders . . . ARMS STRAIGHT FORWARDS . . . and twiddle those fingers to keep them supple.

Richard Hammonds

Start the exercise all over again with hands on the hips and shoulders, but this time stretch your arms SIDEWAYS (be sure to keep the arms level with the shoulders), and twiddle the fingers once more.

. . . and lastly, with one hand on the hip, turn right round from the waist to touch the horse's quarters with the TIPS of the fingers.

But remember that the whole object of these mounted exercises is to help you to become SUPPLE from the waist UPWARDS. Whilst from the waist DOWNWARDS the correct SEAT and LEG position MUST BE MAINTAINED.

(Watch one another carefully and critically, otherwise the whole benefit of the exercises will be lost.)

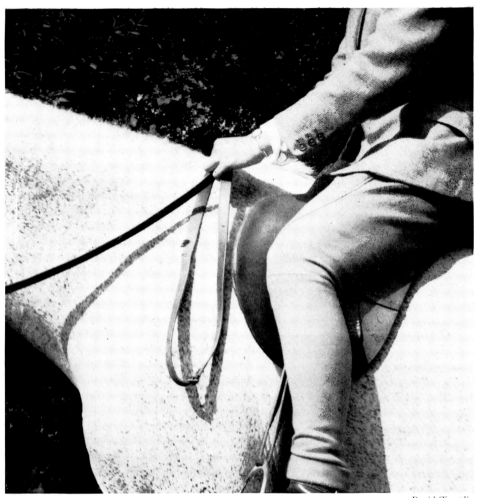

David Tamplin

At long last, a good position mounted.

When you are leading your horse, try slipping your fingers through the noseband of his head collar occasionally.

A lesson that will be very useful later on—as you will see!

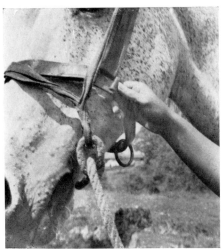

He will soon learn to accept guidance from your fingers as you bring him in from his field.

TURN RIGHT—
A gentle 'feel' to turn his head towards you.

TURN LEFT—
Those quiet fingers just pressed against his cheek.

STOP (HALT)—
A backward pressure on the noseband.

('Only too glad to obey,' says Peter, 'my chance for a snooze!')

4 · *Practising a Better Position Mounted*

Once more this practice on the wall produced the desired results. Pippa could now not only land lightly but:

1. BE READY and POISED to move FORWARD AS THE HORSE MOVED
2. HER ANKLES HAD BECOME SUPPLE so that she was now able to use her calves, and her calf muscles, without turning out her toes duck-wise as before.
3. She was beginning to GAIN STRENGTH IN HER THIGHS.
4. And by CONTINUAL PRACTICE WITH THE REINS, her elbows were becoming more supple and therefore her hands lighter.

So the great day arrived when we felt she was ready to try out all this on Peter. But although she had begun to look and feel quite proficient on the wall, we were obliged to warn her that progress might not run quite so smoothly once she found herself restored to the saddle again. So as a precautionary measure we suggested that for the time being she should invite the services of a kind friend to help her. We asked this friend to walk quietly by Peter's side, slipping her fingers through his nose band, or 'cavason' as it is called, and with the very SOFTEST touch just be ready to apply restraint, if and when it might occasionally be needed. In fact at present this helper would be required to lead and guide Peter entirely—just as Pippa had already taught him to get used to being led as she too slipped

D

her fingers through the nose band of his head collar when leading him backwards and forwards to the field.

By this means—and until Pippa was really expert at sitting in her new position—she would be able to dispense with the reins and concentrate exclusively upon her seat and her legs.

(As many of you perhaps already know, there is another method of thus teaching, re-teaching, or improving a rider's seat and that is by putting the horse on the lunge. So that once again, someone else takes the real control of him while the rider is absolutely free to concentrate upon his own position in the saddle.)

But two essential factors are necessary for this type of instruction—

Firstly—a fit horse.

And *secondly*—AN EXPERT IN CHARGE OF THE LUNGE.

Not everyone is able to conjure up these two essentials at his command. Few amateurs have really fit horses at their disposal and fewer still can find an expert to teach them by this method, nor are purses always long enough to pay for such first-class tuition if indeed it can be found. But any amateur, with almost any type of horse or pony, be it young and green, or stiff and elderly, can soon teach it to understand the 'feel' of being gently guided by a finger in its nose band. And any intelligent and QUIET friend can be employed as such a 'helper'.

So we suggested that a friend of Pippa's should come to her aid now—a friend who needless to say had been very carefully chosen for her quiet tact, interest and patience—and before they started she had been quickly briefed in the gentle art of guiding Peter with this finger in his nose band. (Look at the picture and you will see exactly how it is done.)

And well it was that we had enlisted the services of this 'helper' for when this great day arrived when Pippa was ready to try out her new 'seat' on Peter although, when we brought him out into the yard she landed this time like a veritable feather in the saddle, a look of apprehension quickly spread over her face as though her thoughts travelled back to those painful bangs on the nose that she suffered on the last mounted occasion! Peter, too, had not forgotten. (Horses seldom forget anything, especially their misdemeanours, which they will ALWAYS repeat again ON EXACTLY THE SAME PATCH OF GROUND.)

'Now make ready for a jab in the mouth!' said Peter to himself as he felt Pippa land in the saddle, and up went his head again! But this time Pippa was well prepared and her nose spared another bang for she remembered the advice she had been given soon after Peter had first arrived when, as she tried to lead him from the orchard, he had dug in his heels and thrown up his head in protest. What had she done then? Simply let her fingers slide down the halter rope and allowed his HEAD TO GO.

What did she do now? Exactly the same. She raised her hands and let the reins slip through her fingers and made no attempt whatsoever to pin down Peter's head; and so surprised was Peter to find his mouth unpunished by the expected jab and his head unrestrained by the usual martingale, that he DROPPED HIS NOSE at once to see what was up! Then, as the friend at his side slipped her fingers again through his nose band and spoke quietly to him, he walked sedately out of the yard quite willing and fully prepared to do anything within reason that should be asked of him.

We advised Pippa—until she had become ABSOLUTELY ACCUSTOMED to this new way of sitting and until she WAS COMPLETELY SURE OF HER BALANCE—lest she should interfere again unwittingly in any way with his mouth, TO HOLD ON TO PETER'S MANE. (Another method is to hold on to a neck strap.)

Not only would this save Peter's mouth from any possible sudden jerk, but it would also help Pippa to keep herself in a forward, balanced position and would begin sowing the seeds of the gentle art of KEEPING THE HANDS STILL—a point which is often hard to remember.

For many days we continued this first 'mounted' practice both for Pippa and Peter. We confined ourselves to VERY SHORT practices never more than ten to twenty minutes at a time—so that there would be no chance of Pippa's newly employed muscles being tired and strained, nor should we risk Peter becoming irritated and bored.

In spite of her practice on the wall, Pippa soon discovered that many days were indeed required before she could hope to reach perfection on

Peter's 'moving' back! For just as no ballet dancer can expect to give a finished and polished performance on the stage after two or three afternoons' practice at the bar, so can no rider possibly acquire a perfectly balanced, poised and steady seat, with every muscle under perfect control, after a few hours of exercises either mounted or on a stone wall!

Indeed, how obvious did this become when we asked Pippa's friend to stop Peter suddenly, at intervals, and without warning! How quickly Pippa tended to lurch backwards into her old position again, or wobble sideways at these unexpected and surprise 'halts', and how many jabs in the mouth would the unfortunate Peter have suffered again had she not been HOLDING ON FIRMLY TO HIS MANE.

During these first mounted sessions we frequently reminded Pippa to think about the goal at which she was trying to aim. And lest you too should have forgotten some of the points already mentioned, as we walk slowly round let us repeat them once more. She was aiming to:

1. Keep her weight forward towards the withers, adopting the FEELING OF ALWAYS MOVING FORWARD and thus constantly HELPING and ENCOURAGING the FREE FORWARD MOVEMENT OF THE HORSE.

2. PRESS DOWN INTO THE LOWEST PART OF THE SADDLE, thus strengthening the thigh muscles until by dint of their strength comes an absolutely STEADY seat, poised gracefully over the part of the horse where movement is least accentuated, and where the rider moves only in harmony and rhythm with him.

3. Ensure that with strong thigh muscles and knee acting only as a pivot, the lower leg begins of its own accord to hang naturally over the girth, so that the calves—supple and independent—can maintain JUST the DESIRED contact with the horse's sides; BUT NO MORE: thus being able to SPEAK to him, SOFTLY, GENTLY or more FORCEFULLY, as may be required, in THE ONLY SATISFACTORY language he can be taught to understand.

4. And finally, remember that supple ankles will ensure straight feet whose heels pressed down help to keep the whole body in the correct position; and the balls of the feet—the natural SPRING POINT of the

body—resting on the stirrup irons help the rider imperceptibly to 'spring' forward . . . forward . . . with each step as the horse moves on.

At last, after several days of this first mounted practice, Pippa did appear to have really got her balance. We watched expectantly from afar and were glad to see that however suddenly or unexpectedly Peter might stop Pippa's position never varied. She remained steady: completely still; lightly poised AND READY TO MOVE FORWARD AGAIN.

You try and see if you can achieve these same results!

So the moment had now arrived to try the next step. The next time Peter stopped we suggested that Pippa herself should ask him to move forward again. Not by a 'kick in the ribs' as formerly, but this time with no more than the QUIETEST 'FEEL' with her calves—hardly more than just the tightening of the calf muscles would be required to begin with—for it is as well to remember that it is EASY ENOUGH TO INCREASE the pressure—if required—but it is not always POSSIBLE to soothe the ruffled feelings of a sensitive horse who has suffered far too rude an awakening from too sharp a command at the beginning of a ride! Indeed, he may well bear resentment and be skittish, silly, tiresome and altogether frivolous in just retaliation during the rest of his morning's work.

We reminded Pippa therefore to use THE LEAST POSSIBLE AMOUNT OF LEG when asking Peter to move forward the first time and to INCREASE it GRADUALLY only if necessity really demanded. Pippa carried out instructions to the letter and to her everlasting surprise and astonishment, Peter went on immediately and without the slightest hesitation!

Of course he did! Was he not an old soldier, we explained. He knew perfectly well that when he FELT his rider's weight forward in the saddle they were on the point of MOVING FORWARD, and only the slightest 'feel' of the rider's legs against his sides was enough to confirm this idea.

And now that he was enjoying the additional advantage of finding his HEAD QUITE FREE and his mouth ABSOLUTELY untouched he was so comfortable, so much at ease, that with nothing to upset, fluster or annoy him, he felt perfectly ready and willing to carry out any reasonable request instantaneously.

53

(When you have acquired this same poised and balanced seat, try out these same tactics on almost any horse and you may be certain to find that he too will move forward willingly when he feels this command given by calves alone, even though his whole life has been punctuated by constant bangs from many heels!)

So this further lesson of asking Peter to 'answer to the leg' was, to Pippa's gratification, entirely uneventful. For Peter knew it all already!

There was, of course, an occasion one morning when Peter, hearing a tractor in a nearby field, stopped dead and apparently paid no further heed to Pippa's quiet 'squeeze' asking him to go on again. 'Now may I give him a little kick this time?' she asked somewhat impatiently. 'MOST CERTAINLY NOT!' we warned her. For, as we tried to explain, Peter was NOT DISOBEY-ING her wishes; it was merely that his thoughts were momentarily otherwise engaged! He was simply NOT 'LISTENING' to her.

(One does not pick up a poker and hit one's father over the head if he fails to answer some trivial question through temporary inattention! One just waits POLITELY until his thoughts have returned to earth, and then one tries again.) Just exactly the same applies to a horse. He cannot possibly be expected to PAY FULL ATTENTION to every SINGLE 'remark' his rider makes AT ALL TIMES. His thoughts too are bound to wander and his attention be occasionally diverted by something more interesting at hand. On the contrary it is a good opportunity for the rider himself to 'mend his manners', to wait patiently and then repeat the request POLITELY.

So Pippa did just this:

1. She sat quite still for a minute or two.
2. She allowed Peter to investigate and thoroughly digest the strange sight and sound of the nearby tractor.
3. Then when she instinctively 'FELT' his interest in the tractor flagging, she quickly, tactfully and quietly 'ASKED' with her calves again.

This time Peter's thoughts had reverted once more to his rider. His full attention was again at her disposal. He was 'listening'. He obeyed at once and on he went again perfectly WILLINGLY and AMICABLY.

How different might matters have been had Pippa lost patience and

54

administered a sharp kick! TEMPER, FEAR, OR JUST LACK OF CONFIDENCE ARE THE HORSE'S IMMEDIATE REACTIONS TO A RIDER'S HASTY IMPATIENCE; and how quickly arguments turn to battle and disillusionment sets in so that the harmony and tranquillity, that may have taken many weeks to build, can be uselessly squandered and frittered away in less time than the story takes to tell.

Afterwards there is only one cure to trouble that inevitably arises—ONE HAS TO START ALL OVER AGAIN!

So we counselled Pippa once again NEVER to lose her head or her patience and she would then find that in the long run the squeeze with the leg would always have the desired results; and what is even more delightful, she would also discover that LIGHTER and LIGHTER can that squeeze become as the horse's training or re-education progresses, until in the end little more than a 'thought' travelling down the rider's leg is enough for the horse to interpret the rider's meaning.

Pippa tried to remember all these points as, for a few more days, she continued practising this gentle application of the calf. Then taking the matter yet a step further we finally encouraged her to ask Peter to 'turn' by use of the opposite leg—that is to say left leg to turn right and right leg to turn left.

This she found equally easy for had not Peter received just these instructions all through his long life? The only difference was that in his former home these indications of change of direction had usually been punctuated by the 'heel of a boot' which often made him 'see red' and turn far more swiftly and sharply than his almost 'unseated rider' had bargained for!

And while Pippa was practising this 'Better Position Mounted' Peter, too, had been absorbing another useful lesson.

We were lucky in possessing a circular front drive and while continually walking round it with Pippa on his back, he had been unwittingly accustoming himself to bending his ribs—something that can be irksome, irritating and tiresome in the extreme to a horse who has been used to going straight ahead out hunting all his life and the finer points of whose education have never been considered necessary.

Practising a Better Position Mounted

(Again this is another lesson which can perhaps be better and more quickly taught on the lunge. But when lunging is impractical or unavailable much the same results can be quite satisfactorily obtained by leading the horse on either rein round a circular track, following this if possible by work in an enclosed 'school' where he is obliged to 'bend' as he goes into the corners.)

The first day or two, as we had anticipated, Peter found going round and round the drive by no means to his liking. He went round amicably enough the first time, but when confronted by the request a second time he dug in his toes at the sharp corner at each end of the lawn, rolled his eyes, shook his head and made it quite clear that he had had more than enough; but for the gentle suggestions from the quiet helper at his side (who had, as you may by now guess, been chosen for this role for her patience and tact); but for her fingers on his nose band—which INSTEAD OF TRYING TO FORCE AND RE- STRAIN HIM, simply scratched his cheek sympathetically as she coaxed him along—but for this kind and understanding person whose charming ways he really could hardly resist, Peter would certainly have turned on all his repertoire of old tricks again and made things VERY uncomfortable for Pippa and her friend! As it was, to oblige them both, he consented to trudge round and round once more.

But WE KNEW that he had protested at the sharp corner of the lawn, and tried running out again at the tempting entrance to the stable yard, NOT entirely because he was bored, but really because he found that trying to turn those unaccustomed corners was VERY UNCOMFORTABLE AND THIS IS ONE OF THE REASONS why we kept those first mounted lessons so short. We did NOT wish to try Peter's temper too high by asking him to do some- thing which was causing him discomfort. So it is worth while remembering, when schooling or re-schooling a horse, IF HE BEGINS TO PLAY UP, it is usually either BECAUSE HE DOES NOT UNDERSTAND or because the lesson is painful or uncomfortable.

The cure is NOT TO MAKE HIM GO ON, but on the contrary to allow the lesson to STOP!

This is just what we did. When we saw that Peter was beginning to protest at the corners, we gracefully called it a day and allowed the lesson to come to an end.

And so gradually, each day and without further argument, Peter became more and more resigned to trundling round and round the drive as his neck and ribs became more accustomed to BENDING at each fresh turn. And to ensure that both his sides should become equally supple, we made certain that Pippa's first mounted exercises were carried out equally on either rein (that is to say, going round in opposite directions).

Thus Peter and Pippa practised and perfected together the only BASIS UPON WHICH more advanced riding CAN BE BUILT. This involves:

1. The gradual suppling of the horse.
2. The correct position of the rider in the saddle.

If these instructions are faithfully carried out neither achievement is so very hard to come by.

YOUR LESSON

TEACHING YOUR HORSE TO ACCEPT CONTROL BY PRESSURE ON HIS NOSEBAND

When you are leading your horse backwards and forwards to his field, try slipping your fingers sometimes through the noseband of his head-collar or halter and get him gradually accustomed to accepting guidance and control by the 'feel' of your fingers on his noseband.

If you want him to 'turn left', draw his head gently towards you.

To 'turn right' press the backs of your fingers into his cheek.

And he can quickly be taught to 'stop' and 'stand' if you just raise his head and exert a gentle, backward pressure on the noseband. (Look back at the photos opposite page 49.)

When he is quite used to this try the same thing when he is wearing a bridle, again by slipping your fingers through the cavason or noseband.

It is a lesson that will be VERY *useful. (You will have read how Pippa found it so.) For if you want to improve your seat and adopt a somewhat new position in the saddle you* TOO *may need to do all manner of exercises mounted and if you have to abandon the reins while practising these needless to say someone else must take charge of the horse.*

Almost any kind friend can soon be coached into walking alongside and guiding and controlling him for you by this very simple method of fingers slipped through the noseband.

58

Practising a Better Position Mounted

In addition, this method soon helps to improve his manners. Whereas an amateur, hauling him along by the reins, will very soon have just the reverse effect—not to mention helping to spoil his mouth and his temper into the bargain!

And you will find that any horse, young or old, will quickly learn this lesson for it is—

So clear to him,
So comfortable,
And so VERY, VERY EASY FOR HIM TO UNDERSTAND.

YOUR LESSON

On The Lunge

There is only one other possible way for the rider to learn to improve his seat and practice a better position mounted, without having to control the horse, and that is on the lunge.

But this method calls for—

A fit horse.

Preferably a properly enclosed 'school' (such as you can see in the photograph).

And above all, an EXPERT INSTRUCTOR on the end of the lunge!

These essential factors are by no means within the reach of all. Whereas, as has already been explained, almost any patient and helpful amateur friend can soon master the other method to the benefit, comfort, and satisfaction of all concerned.

Here you can see these essential factors . . .

Richard Hammonds

. . . a 'fit' horse in a properly enclosed 'school' or manège as it is usually called

Richard Hammonds

. . . and expert instructor . . .

... and last but not least—correctly adjusted lunging tackle

5 · Re-making a Hard Mouth

So at last the time arrived when Pippa could be allowed to pick up the reins.

'That will be lovely!' she said. 'For there will be no need for anyone to have to lead Peter any longer.' But alas, Pippa was gravely mistaken; for as she herself would quickly discover, it would be at this stage that the continued help of her patient and long-suffering companion would be even more vital.

As Pippa remembered, teaching Peter to 'answer to the leg'—that is to say to fully understand and quickly respond to instructions 'spoken' to him by the various degrees of pressure of the rider's calves—to teach him to answer to these signals had been child's play. For had he not an intimate knowledge of this 'sign language' already? And had we not soon discovered that PROVIDED THAT HE FELT HIS HEAD FREE and his MOUTH ENTIRELY LEFT ALONE, he was perfectly ready and willing to give us his full attention and to comply with our wishes without fuss or argument?

But now we could no longer leave his mouth quite alone. The time had arrived when no further progress could be made without the use of rein and bit. How was this to be achieved without upsetting the apple cart?

Pippa was obliged to confess that, anxious as she was to be able to dispense with her companion and go off for rides on Peter quite alone, she nevertheless had an uncomfortable premonition that as soon as she picked up those reins she might find herself in trouble! For one thing she could not easily forget that painful bang on the nose that Peter had given her as he threw up his head and the thorny question of the standing martingale cropped up once more. Pippa tentatively suggested the advisability of putting one on, just as an emergency measure, as the dark forebodings of the Huntsman still rang clearly in her ears: 'You take my tip and strap down his head tight with a standing martingale. Then you MIGHT have some hopes of stopping the old rogue!' he had advised.

But we remained adamant. For one thing, as we tried to explain to Pippa, so often a martingale, above all a tight one, is only inclined to enhance the very trouble one wishes to eradicate. For by continual fighting AGAINST this 'artificial' control, or 'artificial aid' as it is called, the horse is apt to DEVELOP the muscles on the UNDERSIDE of his neck just in the very spot where muscles are indeed better left flabby! By continually using the strength of these muscles, the horse does in fact give himself greater POWER to throw up his head with less effort to himself!

Now that Peter had had so many weeks, indeed so many months of comparative inactivity, those muscles had dwindled and lost all their power. The very LAST thing we wished to do, therefore, was in any way to revive their strength!

But more important still, if Pippa were really going to be able to control Peter happily and SAFELY on her own, we must endeavour to find some means whereby she could do so WITHOUT actually having to heave and tug to make him stop! For one had only to look at the two of them together to see at a glance that in a battle of STRENGTH it was Peter who could not help winning hands down every time! We must therefore find some means of teaching Peter to stop when he was told without the rider having to pull the reins. If this could but be happily and successfully achieved no martingale or any other gadget or 'artificial aid' would be required.

Pippa thought this sounded an admirable solution to all difficulties: but alas, a somewhat impossible one! However, as we pointed out, it was this or nothing. For to go galloping round the countryside unable to stop was inadvisable and any attempt of Pippa's to quell Peter by sheer physical strength was equally impractical! So if her dream of riding out safely alone were ever to materialize, 'the battle of strength' must be totally discarded and the 'battle of wits' begun.

Although it all sounded rather ambitious, we asked Pippa to cast her mind back (and perhaps you too, would like to turn back your eyes to Chapter 3) and to see whether she remembered exactly how we had taught Peter successfully so far:

1. To come whenever he was called,
2. To stand still to be mounted.
3. And to answer and obey her wishes, conveyed to him through her legs.

Why had Peter learnt to comply so amicably with these wishes and to consent so agreeably to obey?

Simply because in each case IT HAD BEEN MADE INTERESTING AND PLEASANT FOR HIM TO DO SO.

He had soon learnt to come up when he was called because he knew he would get a palatable reward as soon as he dropped his head into the halter; and what is more, he soon discovered that the erstwhile offending halter was now put so quietly and gently over his head, always carefully avoiding his sensitive ears, that he now no longer disliked or dreaded it.

He had quickly learnt to stand still to be mounted when his young rider landed so lightly upon his back that he hardly noticed her arrival, and while, once again, he was liberally rewarded for his continued good behaviour. Indeed he found these rewards most tasty and satisfactory!

And lastly, Pippa herself, thanks to her improved position in the saddle, was able to convey her leg signals or 'aids' so SOFTLY, QUIETLY and EXPERTLY that Peter's sensitive feelings could in no way be upset or his temper roused, rendering him therefore QUICK TO INTERPRET and perfectly willing to OBEY the sign language WHICH HE SO PERFECTLY UNDERSTOOD.

Now, if we could but find some way of conveying our wishes to him THROUGH THE REINS without having to tug, pull, frighten, UPSET OR IRRITATE HIS TEMPER AND HIS NERVES—if we could find some way of persuading him to ACCEPT his bit, BECAUSE IT WAS EQUALLY PLEASANT

63

AND COMFORTABLE TO DO SO, we felt confident in promising Pippa that she would one day find Peter perfectly safe and easy to manage under all circumstances.

But the task would not be an easy one, we warned. Much patience, perseverance and concentration would be required before Pippa HERSELF could be made to understand what was needed, much less hope to explain this new lesson clearly to Peter!

However, having got so far successfully, Pippa was game to try, even though it did mean many more days spent trundling round our front drive.

As usual, THE FIRST TASK WAS TO TRY TO TEACH THE RIDER, BEFORE THERE WAS ANY HOPE OR POSSIBILITY OF ATTEMPTING TO EXPLAIN OR TEACH SUCH A DIFFICULT NEW LESSON TO THE HORSE.

So we began with Pippa and we tried to paint a picture in her mind's eye of what we hoped to achieve. We asked her to think of a 'door'.

'What an extraordinary idea!' Pippa laughed. 'Think of a door?'

Despite this interruption we struggled on. We asked her to imagine a door —SHUT. Then to think of Peter walking up to this door and finding it shut. What would he do?

'Well, stand still, I suppose, until somebody opened it!' Pippa chuckled.

Exactly! Pippa had already put into words just precisely what we wanted to explain.

Now let us try to think of a way of illustrating this with the reins. We showed Pippa how to hold her reins in a 'square' (which would incidentally and at the same time, teach those wandering hands of hers to KEEP STILL and TOGETHER); so we showed her how to make this 'square' and told her that this was to represent the 'door'. (Look at the photograph.)

Now try to imagine that to shut this door, and to KEEP IT SHUT, Pippa must learn to hold that square ABSOLUTELY STILL.

(This sounded easy enough, but how VERY difficult it was in reality poor Pippa was soon to discover.)

The next step was to try to ask Peter to walk up to that 'door' and then, discovering it shut, he would find himself obliged to stop.

How were we going to do this, we asked Pippa. How could we 'push' Peter up to that 'door'?

'I suppose by squeezing him with my calves as I have been doing already?' Pippa answered quickly enough.

Pippa was partly right, but this time more than just the application of her calves would be needed. Pippa would have to use those back muscles, her thighs, her seat, her weight and, in fact, all weapons at her command to summon enough strength to PUSH Peter up to that 'door' and to 'collect' him, as it is called.

And her hands—that 'square' representing the 'door'—would have to remain QUITE STILL to convey to Peter the idea of that 'door' firmly closed, up against which he was obliged to stop.

It all sounded a little complicated, but Pippa was willing to try. She fully agreed, however, that the continued help of her kind and patient companion would most certainly be sorely needed!

So that morning and for many successive days thereafter, Pippa, Peter and her companion returned to their ambles round our circular drive, in a vain endeavour to master this far harder lesson.

What a fiasco did our 'word picture' prove to be on that first morning that we tried it out! Pippa prepared her reins in the 'square'; she urged Peter forward with her calves, and THOUGHT she was using her back, thighs and seat, not to mention her weight into the saddle as well; but so unaccustomed was she to employing all these extra 'shots in the locker' that all poor Peter felt was something of a prod in his sides, a great deal of uncomfortable wriggling in the saddle, and tightly-held reins which, as soon as he thrust his jaw forward . . . gave . . . gave . . . gave . . . and showed him no 'word picture' at all!

They tried again. Peter's confusion became even greater. Indeed he began to get rather annoyed. What were these two silly girls playing at this time? He had been quite willing to trail round and round the drive every day to please them when his rider sat as still and light as a feather and did nothing more than occasionally ask him to move forward with the gentle application of her legs while the kind companion at his side had continued to guide him by his nose band. He was quite willing and agreeable to continue in this same way. But when tactics changed and he found his rider thumping, wriggling and making things very uncomfortable upon his back and then, to make matters worse, interfering with his mouth as well, his patience and good humour began to desert him.

As we had unfortunately only too clearly foreseen, it was not long before Peter was opening his mouth wide, or 'yawing' as it is called; shaking his head, swishing his tail; and finally pushing Pippa's companion out of the way with his nose in no uncertain manner, nearly knocking her off her feet!

Poor Pippa, both she and her friend began to lose heart. They all seemed to be 'overfaced' this time by a jump too stiff for any of the three to negotiate.

As usual, when these setbacks arose, we tactfully suggested to Peter that his day's work was done and we led him quietly round the drive a time or two to soothe his ruffled feelings and to make sure of returning him to his stable in a more amiable frame of mind.

Next day we began all over again and we tried to encourage Pippa to fresh perseverance by explaining to her that, as usual, most of her difficulties were arising because Peter DID NOT UNDERSTAND.

As Pippa herself was the first to admit, it was hard enough to paint in HER mind's eye this picture of the closed 'door', although we could at least convey our thoughts and ideas to her in human language of the spoken word. Whereas if we wished to explain all this to Peter we had no other means at our disposal than a continual process of 'trial and error' until he eventually tumbled to the idea himself; and being a very intelligent animal, he began to 'feel' what we were driving at.

But how hard this must inevitably be when Peter could in reality neither 'see with his eye' nor absorb through any words this picture of the closed door that we had endeavoured to paint to Pippa. No wonder poor Peter was apt to lose patience and get flustered, irritated, upset and annoyed.

And then there was that other factor to be taken into account. Once more it was the RIDER WHO WAS LARGELY AT FAULT. Pippa, inexperienced and therefore indefinite in her commands, had herself only a hazy idea of what

66

she was trying to teach! No wonder neither teacher nor pupil had made much progress up to date!

We had to try again to make the lesson clearer and simpler for them both. So we pointed out to Pippa that first of all, far from keeping her hands STILL —despite the aid of holding the reins in a 'square'—those reins were in actual fact moving . . . moving . . . moving . . . slightly forward every time she was hoping to ask Peter to stop.

To make this easier we suggested that to begin with, when she wished to hold the reins still, Pippa should press her knuckles firmly down on to Peter's neck and mane. She would then not only be able to FEEL, but actually to SEE if they moved from the original spot.

And to convey more clearly to Peter this idea of stopping at the closed 'door' we asked the helper, too, to concentrate VERY hard and give her usual 'firm feel' on his nose band at one and the same time. (For had not Peter become completely familiar with this 'feel' on the nose band when he was required to stop? For weeks past had not this sign or signal been given to him when he was being led in from the fields, and later while he was being led round and round the drive?)

At the same time Pippa must try to 'push' Peter up to that 'door' far more firmly and expertly, by use of back, seat, thighs, and weight just as— or possibly a split second BEFORE—she held her reins still and her companion at the same time gave Peter that 'feel' on the noseband.

All these efforts in fact, on the part of both Pippa and her companion, must COINCIDE.

How impossible it all seemed at first.

How impossible it so often appears to be to try to explain to a horse, or for that matter to any animal one hopes to train, some point that it is so vital for him to understand. One almost gives up hope. One feels VERY much inclined to give in; and then, quite suddenly, when it has seemed as though the game were not worth the candle, quite suddenly and unexpectedly at the eleventh hour when one has just about decided to give up—just at that VERY moment, 'the penny drops', the pupil miraculously seems to grasp our meaning.

The feeling this gives is one of the most wonderful satisfaction and deep rejoicing.

And this is exactly what happened to Peter and Pippa.

Quite suddenly one morning, as Pippa pushed him with her seatbones, her back, her thighs, up into her calves, and at the same time held those reins SO GENTLY, but SO FIRMLY STILL and her companion gave that 'FEEL' on the noseband at one and the same moment (and for once they managed to achieve all this in perfect unison) quite suddenly Peter STOPPED!

But as Pippa exclaimed with delight and surprise, something even more satisfactory happened at that memorable moment—Pippa experienced an abrupt, quite unexpected and wholly delightful sensation. It was, she explained, as though Peter's whole head seemed to 'GIVE' when he felt that SOFT, STILL REIN (that invisible 'closed door') preventing him from going any farther.

Peter had indeed 'GIVEN'. He had in fact accepted at long last the control of the bit and rein and had, to all intents and purposes, quite literally GIVEN HIMSELF UP WITH CONFIDENCE into the now gentle and capable hands of his rider, as at long last he began fully to understand her meaning.

He finally realized that when he felt her PUSH HIM STRONGLY FORWARD into that soft but FIRMLY HELD REIN, he was, quite simply, just expected TO STOP!

And when he had at last discovered that this command was apparently no longer to be preceded by a hauling and tugging at the reins and unbearable discomfort to his mouth (not to mention an insult to his feelings!) when this new realization suddenly dawned upon him, so thankful was he, that in sheer gratitude he positively sighed with relief and allowed himself to relax completely.

Which was just what we had been waiting for.

He had in fact RELAXED HIS JAW!

(You try all these tactics with your horse and if you, too, will but persevere with equal fortitude and patience, so will he also, in the end, tumble to the idea and thankfully 'give' and relax. And what a happy achievement it is for both parties concerned!)

Re-making a Hard Mouth

How worth while had been all these patient hours of trial and error, practice and perseverance! But before we allowed Pippa to dismount and Peter to make tracks for his comfortable stable, we asked Pippa and her companion to pause for a moment and reflect upon one final point. We asked them to look carefully at the exact patch of ground where this miracle had taken place!

They looked and pondered and between them they noticed that Peter had been approaching a CORNER of the drive and had BEEN FACING VERY SLIGHTLY UPHILL.

And herein lies another secret of success when striving to achieve this lesson. It is usually easier to EXPLAIN to a horse how to relax his jaw, and one is often more likely to obtain success, if one tries at first when his head happens to be VERY slightly turned to one side and if possible when he is facing slightly uphill. Once he has understood and relaxed his jaw this way, it is only a question of continued and patient practice to get him to respond equally well when moving straight ahead.

And so that triumphant morning, as they were soon to appreciate, both Pippa and Peter had tumbled to and understood the foundation of all future obedience and control and the only satisfactory method of re-making a hard mouth.

It is called FLEXION.

YOUR LESSON

Learning to Stop Correctly—(Or Collectedly)

When you have so practised and perfected the correct position in the saddle, and have such balance and control of your own *body that you find you are able to indicate your wishes to your horse, not only through the lightest variations of the usual 'leg aids', but also through the use of your seat bones and the adjustment of your weight. . . .*

And when your horse has become more supple, responsive and co-operative both in body AND MIND *(as you will find he will become if you have been carrying out these exercises correctly and your helper playing her part intelligently with her fingers slipped through his nose band), and he will obey more quickly these messages 'spoken' to him by this means and is ready and willing to go instantly* FORWARD. . .

Then has the moment arrived to take up your reins again and ask him TO STOP!

But this you must learn to do NOT BY PULLING AT THE REINS, *but by the more advanced method of* PUSHING HIM UP INTO HIS BIT *and persuading him to relax his jaw.*

This can be very difficult.

Instead of pulling the horse back, you must try to PRESS HIM FORWARD *into a still—or unyielding—rein, as it is called. You must learn to push him forward, up into his bridle and up against that still, quiet rein that forms a barrier past which he finds he cannot go.*

So he is obliged TO STOP!

And to prevent the rein from yielding, the rider's hands must, of necessity, be held STILL.

Richard Hammonds

To ask your horse to 'Stop' or 'HALT' correctly —and 'collectedly'—means, NOT PULLING HIM BACK, but PUSHING HIM FORWARD instead, into a still, or unyielding rein.

To prevent the reins from yielding—or from moving or 'giving'—is FAR more difficult than it sounds!

But it does help to begin with if you hold your reins in a 'square' like this. (Study the photos.)

Across the palm of your hand . . .

Richard Hammonds

. . . and together,

(When the square is formed watch carefully to make sure that both reins are of exactly equal length. Keep them so, by the thumbs pressed firmly on the reins.)

Richard Hammonds

. . . thus forming a 'square'.

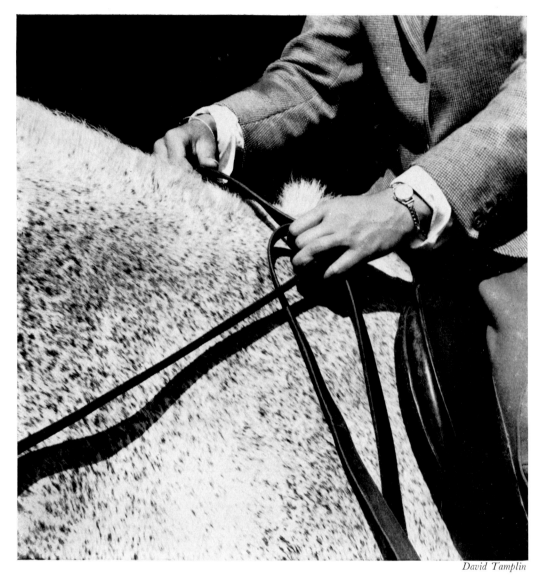

Also to start with if the hands be held DOWN—with the backs of the fingers just 'feeling' against the horse's neck—this does help the rider to get the idea of keeping STILL HANDS.

(Later, when the rider becomes more expert, it will be found easy to maintain a 'still rein' with the hands raised in the usual way.)

Re-making a Hard Mouth

To keep the hands quite still is far less simple than it sounds. But to start with, it tends to help matters if the reins are held in a square just as you see in the picture.

Once again, you may well find that your horse will tumble to the idea before you can really put the movement properly into practice! And this is where that kind helper, with her fingers slipped through his noseband, again becomes invaluable. Her pressure on the nose band at the appropriate moment soon makes it clear to the horse what you are trying to get him to do, and in next to no time he will be only too thankful to respond to your new signals 'to stop' this way because it is so much more COMFORTABLE *for him to do so and in gratitude he will soon learn to* RELAX HIS JAW. . . . WHICH IS THE WHOLE OBJECT OF THE EXERCISE!

(And incidentally, the only satisfactory way of re-making a hard, or unresponsive mouth.)

ABOUT PIPPA AND PETER

6 · *Work at the Walk*

But although this longer and very much harder lesson of teaching Peter to relax his jaw and of trying to show Pippa how to obtain or ask for 'flexion' had at last been mastered, the lesson, far from being completed, had only just been tentatively begun.

As Pippa herself had by now already anticipated, and as you too perhaps have guessed, many more long hours of practice would be required before Pippa could be really certain that Peter would not only understand, but would willingly OBEY this new form of control INSTANTLY and UNDER ALL CIRCUMSTANCES.

Just as he had once stood stock still and failed to 'listen' to the instructions given him through the legs when his thoughts were otherwise and more actively engaged (if you have forgotten about this turn back again to Chapter 4, page 54)—just as Peter had failed to 'listen' to these leg signals so, as Pippa was soon to discover, there would be many an occasion when he would, through inattention or possibly through fright, fail utterly to respond to this new form of control through the reins.

Instead of relaxing his jaw, fear, worry, or irritation would send his thoughts to the winds and he would 'LOSE HIS MOUTH' again, as it is called; in fact he would yaw, pull, shake his head and revert to all his old failings once more. And the only way we could put him to the test and invite these situations of fear, irritation, boredom or just inattention to arise, was to forsake the now all too familiar tranquillity of our home drive and take Peter further afield.

'Then at long last I can go out on my own?' sighed Pippa with relief.

But once more we were obliged to tell her she was doomed to further disappointment. For this new lesson was, as yet, as fragile as a cobweb in Peter's mind and should he be ALLOWED to pull again, AND GET AWAY WITH IT, back they would have to come to the garden once more where, with the patience and tenacity of a spider, that lesson would have to be re-woven all over again like a veritable web.

Pippa agreed that this would be a strain that even her patience could hardly be expected to bear and she admitted that she would prefer to continue to seek the help of her companion at Peter's head and postpone this much-longed-for day of taking Peter out quite alone, rather than risk any setbacks in their joint progress now that they had managed to travel so far along the road to success.

But if her companion were still needed and was to come with her how was she going to keep up? Pippa enquired. That was easy to answer, for Pippa and Peter were at present to confine themselves to THE WALK!

For as Pippa was to learn (and you perhaps already know) the 'Walk' is a four-time pace, slow, measured and sedate and the finest pace for the training—or re-training—of both horse and rider.

You can see in the diagram on page 78 how the horse's foot-falls occur (or their 'sequence' as it is called); and if you look at it carefully you will also notice that never, at any time, has the horse got fewer than two feet on the ground; sometimes he has three taking all his weight while only one foot at a time is poised in the air.

This means that with his weight so comfortably and evenly distributed there is little or no strain on the horse's legs, yet while he is thus walking quietly, tendons and ligaments and the muscles all over his body soon begin to harden and strengthen, so that with no undue effort it is not long before he is feeling 'fighting fit'. This is why 'The Walk' is accepted and acknowledged as the finest pace for putting on 'condition'—as getting hard, fit and ready for faster work is called.

The rider, too, feels little motion as they saunter quietly along; for the four-time pace of 'The Walk' being slow and tranquil, the effort is slight and both body and mind tend to remain calm, unruffled, relaxed and composed. Thus at this pace both horse and rider have every opportunity of getting to know one another better; to improve their training, or re-training; to learn to give and receive; to ask for and to obey; and to practise together, each time they go out, every lesson so far attempted and learnt.

'The Walk' is, in fact, the finest pace in which to consolidate all gains!

So Pippa and Peter now spent many happy days walking round the lanes together, their kind companion still trudging cheerfully at Peter's side lest anything should startle or upset him, then with fingers ready to take a quick hold of that nose band again, they could ensure that in a moment of distraction Peter would never be permitted to taste the pleasure of pulling once more! And we advised Pippa to retain the services of her companion until she herself felt quite confident that they were no longer really needed.

While they were so engaged, Pippa discovered several interesting things. She noticed for instance—

1. That as she allowed Peter to walk along on a fairly loose rein he gradually began to stretch out his neck and lower his head, thus eradicating completely and of his own accord that tiresome habit of throwing up his head at the slightest provocation and hitting her on the nose. (Pippa had in fact stumbled upon the knowledge that to make a horse stride out at the walk helps in itself to 'position' his head correctly.)

2. That the farther he stretched out his neck the more comfortable his paces became. He seemed to move more smoothly with a delightful slow, rhythmical swing, and yet get along faster. He was in fact beginning to 'lengthen his stride', as it is called.

And in order to help to encourage and enhance this excellent new development we gave Pippa a tip. We told her to watch Peter's shoulders as he walked. First his right shoulder would swing forward, as his 'off fore' came to the ground; then his left shoulder would stretch out in front of her as his 'near fore' advanced; and as we wanted to HELP and ASSIST him to LENGTHEN HIS STRIDE—rather than to scuttle along and increase his pace —Pippa would find that if, instead of pressing him on to further efforts by dint of a squeeze from BOTH her calves at once, she used ALTERNATE CALVES as he walked along, she would soon discover that he was really striding out to his fullest possible capacity.

You try this. But like everything else it requires a little patience and practice and it is useless to attempt it UNTIL THE RIDER'S SEAT IS CORRECT, and his thighs, seatbones and the strength of his back are all playing their allotted parts. Then he must accustom himself, by careful observation, to seeing which shoulder IS IN FACT MOVING FORWARD, so that he knows EXACTLY which foreleg is ABOUT TO TOUCH THE GROUND.

Then, having mastered these details, the rider must apply the RIGHT leg as the horse's near shoulder moves forward and his LEFT leg as the horse's off shoulder advances.

After a little practice Pippa soon discovered she could do this and quickly found for herself the marked improvement it began to make in Peter's continued and CONSISTENT lengthening of stride.

So their outings continued happily together until Pippa found that not only could she make him walk out to full capacity at will, but she could also be certain of stopping him whenever she wished. So gradually she dispensed with her companion's services and how happy was the thought that at long last—even if the pace were only at 'The Walk'—she could take Peter out quite alone, having every confidence that she had complete control of him.

Sometimes as they passed through the village she would meet a friend and want to stop for a chat and how wonderful and almost exhilarating was the knowledge that, by pushing Peter UP and INTO his bridle in the approved fashion, just a finger-light touch on that STILL REIN was enough to stop him dead at the appropriate moment. While no more than a

75

'thought' travelling down her calves sent him walking quietly on again when gossip with the passer-by was ended.

How worthwhile had been these patient days of concentrated effort, for what more gratifying and wholly satisfactory sensation can there be than when a horse and rider feel IN TUNE!

YOUR LESSON

Learning To Understand 'The Walk'

At last, after all this practice in some enclosed place near home or in your 'school', the time will arrive to ride out farther afield; and it will greatly help you to improve your riding if you have a clear understanding of just how your horse is moving under you.

So here are some drawings which may help you to picture his movements in their most simplified form.

As it is so essential to try to realize that your horse must first be PUSHED *forward,* BY YOU, *up and on to his bit—before he moves at all—all these movements are portrayed as beginning from* BEHIND—*the seat of his locomotion as it were.*

Watch and listen carefully to his hoof beats and you will find that 'The Walk' is a four-time movement with an even, rhythmical beat. . . .

'Off Hind . . . followed by . . . Off Fore.

'Near Hind . . . followed by . . . Near Fore.

'One . . . Two . . . Three . . . Four.

'Clip . . . Clop . . . Clipety . . . Clop.'

Stand directly behind your horse as he walks along and you will notice the swing of his tail from side to side, just like the even, rhythmical swing of a clock's pendulum.

A good swing to the tail denotes a long stride and the ability to gallop fast.

When you are riding him, you yourself can help him to lengthen that stride by pushing him along and encouraging him to walk out to his full capacity by use of ALTER-

77

THE WALK

1. OFF HIND FORWARD

2. OFF FORE FORWARD.

3. NEAR HIND FORWARD.

4. NEAR FORE FORWARD.

NATE *leg 'aids'—or leg pressure. Allow him plenty of length of rein; watch the movement of his shoulders carefully; and as his* NEAR *fore comes forward and to the ground, apply your opposite,* RIGHT *leg; as his* OFF *fore advances, apply your* LEFT *leg.*

If you manage to do this correctly you should soon feel the swing and the rhythm as he strides out better. But if he just seems to scuttle along faster you will know that you have not quite understood these directions! Try again.

If things go wrong it may well be your hands that are at fault. Watch them carefully, and watch your horse's head too and you will notice that at this four-time beat of 'The Walk' his head advances and recedes very slightly; in and out; backwards and for-wards; rather like the movement of a wave on the seashore. So must YOUR HANDS *gently follow this movement of the head; backwards and forwards; give and take.*

Otherwise, if you hold your reins tight and rigid at 'The Walk' you will impede your horse's progress and he will be forced to scuttle faster instead of stretching out his neck and lengthening his stride.

ABOUT PIPPA AND PETER

7 · *Faster Paces*

So now that work at 'The Walk' had really reached satisfactory completion and Pippa felt she had absolute acquiescence and control; and Peter, thanks to all this slow work, was feeling 'fighting fit' and 'up on his toes', the time had arrived when we could safely concentrate upon faster paces and the next one of course to be tackled was 'The Trot'.

Look again at the diagram and you will see (if you do not already know) that 'The Trot' has a two-time beat. Diagonally placed legs rise and fall alternately.

This very rhythm—one, two, one, two—speaks for itself of smart, slick, pent-up energy, like a spring wound tightly, ready to be uncoiled.

So the fit horse gathers himself together for action by raising his head and arching his neck in a concentration of his energy, veritably 'collected' together, as he springs first from one pair of legs to the other.

And in order to help enhance and ASK the horse to change from the leisurely saunter of 'The Walk'—where the rider's hands have no option but to move gently backwards and forwards as the horse's head advances and recedes with his long, four-beat strides—in order to help and encourage the horse to summon all his energy to change to 'The Trot', the rider must himself help to 'collect' him by—

1. Shortening the reins.

2. Keeping them STILL, SHORT and INFLEXIBLE.
3. And at one and the same time pressing the horse into action and, as usual, UP TO THE BIT, by vigorous use of BOTH calves.

Pippa faithfully tried out all these instructions and soon she had Peter, despite his advanced years, changing quickly and smartly from walk to trot as he felt her give him the required 'aids'.

But then how to slow down again?

Once more, NEVER—NEVER—by PULLING AT THE REINS!

On the contrary, if we think it out, to RETURN TO THE WALK the horse must of necessity deflate his energy again as it were—like letting the air out of a hard-blown tyre. To do this he must LOWER his head and neck, in order to be able to relapse into his LONGER, more OUTSTRETCHED walking stride.

Therefore it stands to reason that if, in order to slow down, the rider PULLS AT THE REINS, HE SIMPLY KEEPS THE HORSE'S HEAD UP AND HIS NECK RESTRICTED, making it virtually impossible for him to do as he is asked.

Instead the rider must give a steady 'feel' on the reins AS THE FIRST SIGNAL that the pace is about to decrease, and THEN LET THE REINS GRADUALLY SLIP THROUGH THE FINGERS, while at the same time sitting down firmly in the saddle.

The horse will as a result, and of his own accord, stretch out his neck and resume his stately walk again. Pippa tried out these directions as she rode along and after the far harder lessons that had gone before she found it this time child's play to master.

So we suggested that she should try to acquire the art of the sitting trot.

Again Pippa must endeavour to POISE herself over that spot near the withers where motion, even at the trot, is least accentuated and soon she would discover that she could sit down comfortably in the saddle, especially if she made sure that Peter kept up a steady and pronounced rhythm—one, two—one, two.

We advised her to sing a little song to Peter as they trotted along—'One,

F

two, buckle my shoe, Three, four, knock at the door.' How easily then would the rhythm be kept, and how Peter would enjoy the music!

To start with Pippa tried this out along the flat country road and it did not take long before she could sit down comfortably in the saddle and both she and Peter were well and truly trotting in perfect harmony.

Then we told Pippa to return to the old method and rise up and down again. But this time she must do so with a difference—she must REMEMBER TO CHANGE DIAGONALS at carefully regulated intervals.

What does this mean? Just in case you, like Pippa, are not quite clear, study again the diagram.

As we noticed before, at 'The Trot' the diagonally opposite legs come down to the ground together. So if the rider RISES to the trot he must, of necessity, SIT DOWN IN THE SADDLE as legs 'A' touch the ground and stay UP IN THE AIR as legs 'B' come to earth. Now it does not require much imagination to guess that if the rider ALWAYS SITS DOWN WHILE the pair of legs 'A' are in action and is himself ALWAYS IN THE AIR as legs 'B' are on the ground, naturally poor-pair-of-legs 'A' bear all the weight and strain, while legs 'B' have a very easy time!

If this unhappy state of affairs is allowed to continue too long the horse, sooner or later, may become lame in the two legs—or at all events in one of them—that have been called upon to do all the hard work.

(This is why in some countries riders are always made to keep to a sitting trot on a young horse so that there can be no risk of two of his legs being called upon to bear more strain than the other pair. And it is why horses in harness can often work longer, more happily and better into their old age and remain sounder, because they have no untutored rider posting up and down continually upon the same diagonal!)

So in order to avoid all these troubles the more advanced rider must learn to distribute his weight evenly upon both pairs of legs at the trot; and he does this quite simply by:

1. Rising up and down for perhaps five minutes while pair-of-legs 'A' come to the ground and then
2. Changing over by BUMPING ONCE in the saddle, thus throwing himself

82

on to the pair-of-legs 'B' as they come to the ground. And then up and down he goes again.

You try this . . . Up-down . . . Up-down . . . Up-down . . . BUMP . . . Down-up . . . Down-up . . . Down-up . . . BUMP!

It is quite simple, and as Pippa quickly discovered, you soon know when you have changed as the horse feels quite 'different' on the second diagonal —more especially so if he has become accustomed to his rider continually rising on one side only. Indeed so uncomfortable and peculiar does the change of diagonals feel to him, as well as to the rider, that if he be an 'old soldier', he may try to bump his rider back again on to the more favoured pair of legs by every kind of trick and ruse, including a spell of quite un-called-for shying!

But as he becomes accustomed to the feel of it, so the pair of legs that have been doing the least work become more active again and the change from one diagonal to the other feels, to the rider, less pronounced.

Pippa tried and practised this until she, too, began to be quite adept at changing diagonals and Peter resigned to yet a new sensation in his old age!

So when Pippa and Peter had become thoroughly familiar with, and accustomed to, every angle and aspect of 'The Trot' we opened the gate leading to a seven-acre meadow one morning and sent them out at last across the green grass to enjoy a good canter.

Pippa steered Peter through the gateway with no little trepidation. Although she now felt completely at ease on his back while they had stuck to the roads, and quietly confident that she could manage him perfectly under all circumstances and confronted by any hazards, would she still have just as much control over him with his head turned to open spaces?

But we assured her she need have no fear for we sincerely hoped and guessed that after all these long weeks of patient work and carefully planned re-schooling, such notions as setting off full gallop as soon as he set hoof to turf had, slowly but irrevocably, receded from Peter's innermost thoughts.

And sure enough, as Pippa gave him the correct 'aids', he changed his pace smoothly and away they went out of sight, only to return triumphant as Pippa found him as easy to pull up from a canter as he had been to stop at the walk.

But before we had opened that field gate and let them in, we had briefed Pippa as to how to proceed. She had been told that to change CORRECTLY from TROT to CANTER she must remember a few things—

1. To PREPARE for this change of pace the rider must, as an introduction, remember to STOP RISING UP AND DOWN and revert to a SITTING TROT.

2. Which, if he sits well down in the saddle and again brings all forces at his command to bear in the shape, as usual, of seat, back, thighs and calves and AT THE SAME TIME retains a SHORT, TAUT and STEADY rein, will help the horse to get his hind legs well under him and thus enlist all HIS spare energy for, quite literally, bouncing himself into this faster pace.

3. In fact, TO CHANGE TO ANY FASTER PACE requiring more exertion on the part of the horse, the rider must himself help to supply this extra energy by putting all HIS OWN STRENGTH into gathering the horse together, or 'collecting' him, as it is called. By sitting down in the saddle he is far better able to do so when changing to a canter from 'The Trot'.

Pippa was by now beginning to understand this question of 'collection' and how to encourage and obtain it, and she found this change from trot to canter, following these instructions, very easy to accomplish.

In fact thanks to all these weeks of concentration; trial and error; practice and hard work, she was beginning to find any aspect of more advanced riding comparatively easy and possible to come by.

So that when a kind friend, who had been watching her progress on Peter, was so favourably impressed that she invited Pippa to borrow a young pony and take it to gain experience at a Pony Club Camp, Pippa not only glowed with inward pride, but felt happily confident that she was now quite competent to accept.

There she learnt many new things: how to lead off correctly on a given leg at the canter; how to execute a simple turn on the forehand; how to join in and enjoy, with a fair amount of accuracy, many school movements in conjunction with others in a class; and how to sample the thrill of popping light-heartedly over jumps which had now become pleasurably simple instead of very haphazard.

But perhaps the point that impressed her most—as she confessed to us afterwards—was that she could now 'feel' how much this younger pony had still to learn if his education was to be complete and what long hours SOMEONE would have to spend in teaching him. FOR PERFECTION IN EQUITATION CAN NEVER BE REACHED BY SHORT CUTS.

And how glad she was to return to her own responsive Peter, who had learnt to answer and obey, happily, generously and willingly, her lightest touch and least behest.

YOUR LESSON

Learning To Understand 'The Trot'

In direct contrast to the measured and leisurely tread of 'The Walk', this is a lively, airy-fairy pace when, with head held high and tail cocked, the horse should spring cheerfully from one diagonal pair of legs to the next.

Thus 'The Trot' has a two-time beat:

'Near Hind . . . and Off Fore . . . forward together.'

'Off Hind . . . and Near Fore . . . forward together.'

   One . . . Two . . .

   One . . . Two . . .

   Clip . . . Clop . . .

   Clip . . . Clop . . .

Listen carefully to this hoof-beat as your horse trots along the road and make sure that the rhythm is absolutely precise and even. If it sounds uneven—slow one minute and fast the next—again it may well be your hands that are at fault.

This time exactly the opposite applies. Whereas in 'The Walk' you must let your hands follow the movement of your horse's head to enable him to relax, stretch out his neck and saunter along, when you want him to change from walk to trot you must SHORTEN *your reins; press him up into his bridle; (so indicating to him that he must* COLLECT *himself and summon up all his energy to spring into the trot); and you must* KEEP THOSE REINS SHORT, *still and taut, to help him to maintain this 'collection'.*

Then, if you have managed to carry out these instructions correctly, he should bounce gaily along at a steady, two-time beat.

Faster Paces

But do not forget that when you want him to change back to a walk you must gradually relax and LENGTHEN *the reins again so that he may* LOWER *his head, stretch out his neck and relapse—or collapse—back again into that leisurely, four-time stride.*

And remember to SIT DOWN IN THE SADDLE *to emphasize exactly what you want him to do.*

CHANGING DIAGONALS

Having persuaded your horse to trot correctly—or collectedly—you must next begin to think about easing the burden of your weight upon his back by learning to distribute this weight evenly and alternately on both diagonal pairs of legs—or 'change the diagonal' as it is called.

You can see by the diagram that when rising up and down at 'The Trot' you may find yourself sitting down in the saddle every time pair of legs 'B' comes to the ground and rising up in the air when pair of legs 'A' is in action. If you are going to do this all the time it stands to reason that the 'B' pair of legs will be called upon to do all the work and bear all the strain.

So to change your weight over, bounce once in the saddle. Then you will find yourself sitting down on the 'A' pair of legs instead.

You will read in the text how Pippa learnt to do this. If she could manage it . . . so can you!

THE SITTING TROT

And lastly you must practise the 'sitting trot': NOT *just slouching on the back of the saddle, sliperty-sloperty . . . jog . . . jog . . . jog . . . ! But learning to perch forwards and 'go with your horse', in a lightly balanced position which makes it just as easy for him to keep that even, cheerful, rhythmical hoof-beat as when you are rising up and down.*

Count as you go . . .

　　　　　'One . . . two . . . one . . . two . . .'

Practise the sitting trot hard. Because, as you will soon discover, it is VERY, VERY *important.*

THE TROT

1. NEAR HIND AND OFF FORE FORWARD TOGETHER.

2. OFF HIND AND NEAR FORE FORWARD TOGETHER.

Here you see Pippa again. She is manfully struggling to carry out suggestions to see if she can persuade Peter to stop correctly—and collectedly. (Turn back to page 70 to revise your memory.)

Notice that her friend is still walking alongside with fingers slipped through Peter's noseband ready to apply pressure at the appropriate moment if she can and so help him to understand what his very inexperienced little rider is driving at!

No luck here!
(Because Pippa is still PULLING BACK.)

David Tamplin

Here she is a trifle more successful. Although, as can be seen, she is not using quite enough strength of back and leg to get Peter's hind quarters under him.

But at least he has stopped WILL-INGLY, QUIETLY and COMFORTABLY, having been pushed UP and INTO a STILL REIN instead of being HAULED BACK with an almighty TUG!

David Tamplin

THE TROT

Richard Hammonds

Here you see a well-known instructress demonstrating some points worth remembering about 'The Trot'.

Look carefully at her horse's movements.

As you can plainly see, his OFF FORE and NEAR HIND are RAISED TOGETHER as he trots on. Whilst his DIAGONALLY OPPOSITE pair of legs are still on the ground.

Notice too that he is circling to the LEFT and his rider is SITTING DOWN in the saddle—thus throwing weight and work on the INNER hind leg. (Which is usually acknowledged as being the more satisfactory.)

When the rider 'changes the rein'—trotting diagonally across the 'school' to the opposite corner in preparation for circling in the other direction—(in this case to the right, or on the OFF rein) she will 'change the diagonal' as she rides across so that when circling the other way she will again be putting her weight on the INNER hind leg.

(Puzzle this out, and see if you can do likewise!)

But remember, the most important point is to learn to know which diagonal you are riding on.

THE TROT

Richard Hammonds

And here the instructress demonstrates how to REVERT back again from TROT to WALK.

(NOT by leaning forwards and tugging as hard as possible, which only forces the poor horse to arch his neck even more, and scuttle along all the faster!)

But by SITTING DOWN IN THE SADDLE and quietly and gradually LENGTHENING the reins, so that the horse may stretch out his neck and relapse of his own accord into the more leisurely and sedate pace of 'The Walk' again.

You try—and you will find how quickly your horse learns to obey and how thankfully he responds to correct directions which are, at the same time, POSSIBLE for him to carry out!

THE SITTING TROT

An expert exponent of the art of dressage kindly pauses for a moment during her morning's work in her home paddock to show us the position she adopts for the 'Sitting Trot'. Note carefully her seat; legs; hands; and length of rein.

Notice the spurs too. These are necessary for greater precision in more advanced work.

One day, when YOUR riding has greatly improved, you too may need spurs for advanced work and schooling. But you will find it difficult if not impossible to use them correctly if your foot is wrongly placed and sticking out sideways due to stiff ankles!

David Tamplin

So turn back and study those ankles exercises again and make sure that your ankles are SUPPLE.

(And always remember that . . . SPURS MISUSED ARE SPURS ABUSED.)

Richard Hammonds

Do you recognize this young rider?

She seems to be giving quite a creditable performance at a first attempt at the 'Sitting Trot'.

Turn back and see if you can find her again and see what her riding was like before she conscientiously practised all these exercises and faithfully carried out all these instructions.

(If she can improve HER riding, so can you!)

CHANGING DIAGONAL
AT THE TROT

1. 'A' LEGS ON GROUND,
RIDER RISES UP.

2. 'B' LEGS ON GROUND,
RIDER SITS.

3. RIDER **BUMPS** WHILE
'A' LEGS ARE ON GROUND.

4. 'B' LEGS ON GROUND.
RIDER RISES.

G

Learning To Understand 'The Canter'

As has already been explained on page 77 ALL *movement starts from* BEHIND
and 'The Canter' is no exception to this rule. Here then is the correct sequence. . . .

  1. The OUTSIDE *hind leg moves forward.*
  2. The INSIDE *hind leg and* OUTSIDE *foreleg go forward together.*
  3. Followed by the INSIDE *foreleg (known as the 'leading leg').*

*The canter is a pleasant movement that covers more ground than 'The Trot' but
at a more leisurely and comfortable pace, just like that of an amiable rocking-horse.
Backwards and forwards we go in* THREE-TIME—*first one hind leg, then the opposite
diagonal pair of legs together (exactly as in 'The Trot') and lastly the leading foreleg.*

One	Two	Three
One	Two	Three
Clop	Clopity	Clop
Lop	Lopity	Lop

To keep an even rhythm, count out loud or hum a tune to your horse as you canter along.

*(And study the drawings carefully as they will help you to understand how your
horse is placing his leg beneath you and which foreleg should be leading according to
the direction in which you are going.)*

*But once again it is as well to remember that although falling into a canter may
seem effortless to you, to* CHANGE SMOOTHLY *from Trot to Canter requires a great
deal of exertion on the part of the horse and, as usual, it is* YOU, *the rider, who
must enable him to supply this extra energy by helping him to collect himself before*

he changes pace. This you can only do by sitting down in the saddle and, once again, using your thighs, legs, seat and the strength of your back in unison.

Therefore before attempting to change from Trot to Canter SHORTEN YOUR REINS; *stop rising up and down; and* SIT DOWN IN THE SADDLE *so that you are in the right position to help your horse to get his hind legs well under him.*

And herein lies the advantage of having first perfected yourself at the SITTING TROT!

Then there is another aspect of the canter to be reckoned with. Sometimes you will want the horse to lead with the Near Fore, while at other times the Off Fore leading will be necessary. For remember, when riding a circle, or turning a corner, the INNER *foreleg must always lead. Otherwise your horse is liable to cross his forelegs and come a nasty cropper!*

To ask him to lead with the given foreleg you must use diagonal aids. That is to say, in leading with the NEAR FORE *you will need emphasis on the* NEAR REIN *(or left rein), and your* RIGHT *leg. You will also find it very much easier if, to start with, you ride him on a slight halfcircle, or turning an imaginary corner. Thus when asking him to lead off with the Near Fore, start off on a slightly* LEFT-HANDED BEND. *And to get him to strike off on his Off Fore, turn in a wide sweep slightly to the* RIGHT.

Very soon, and if your diagonal aids have been clearly and correctly given, you will find that your horse will understand and strike off obediently, with either foreleg leading, even though you may be cantering in a straight line.

You try.

Then there is one more point to consider. Study the diagram again carefully and you will notice that although 'The Canter' may be a comfortable, rocking-horse sensation for the rider, it nevertheless means a great strain on the horse. For there are split-second moments when nearly the whole weight of his own and his rider's body rest pivoted on his one leg touching the ground.

Have a care therefore to ask your horse to canter whenever possible ONLY ON SOFT GROUND.

THE CANTER

OFF FORE LEADING
(CIRCLING TO THE RIGHT)

1. NEAR HIND FORWARD
(OUTSIDE HIND LEG)

2. OFF HIND AND NEAR
FORE...FORWARD TOGETHER
(INSIDE HIND LEG AND OUT-
SIDE FORELEG)

3. LASTLY...OFF FORE FORWARD
THE LEADING LEG
(INSIDE LEADING FORELEG)

THE CANTER

NEAR FORE LEADING
(CIRCLING TO THE LEFT)

1. OFF HIND FORWARD
(OUTSIDE HIND LEG)

2. NEAR HIND AND OFF
FORE ·· FORWARD TOGETHER
(INSIDE HIND LEG AND
OUTSIDE FORELEG)

3. LASTLY ··· NEAR FORE FORWARD
<u>THE LEADING LEG</u>
(INSIDE LEADING FORELEG)

YOUR LESSON

LEARNING TO UNDERSTAND 'THE GALLOP'

Away we go at 'The Gallop'! A fast, exhilarating pace, when the horse stretches out neck and tail and down to earth he goes, literally as fast as he can run. For 'The Gallop', although another FOUR-TIME-PACE *like 'The Walk', instead of being a gentle saunter is in fact a glorification of 'The Canter' split up into a run. . . .*

Here, then, is the sequence. . . .

    1. The outside hind leg.

    2. and 3. The inside hind leg (quickly followed by) the outside foreleg.

    4. Lastly the inside foreleg.

(Once again study the picture carefully and you will soon understand.)

And think of the rhythm in FOUR-TIME

One	Two Three	Four
One	*Two Three*	*Four*
Thud	*Thud Thud*	*Thud*
Thud	*Thud Thud*	*Thud*

But when galloping there is one more important point to bear in mind. It does not require great imagination to realize that the strain borne by the horse's one leg, as once again it is called upon for that split-second to take the whole weight of his own and his rider's body is, AT THIS SPEED, *far greater.*

Therefore enjoy your enthusiasm for galloping within reason, but NEVER WITH ABUSE, *and remember that a good gallop is 'heady wine' for a well-bred, fit and high-couraged horse and many need restraint rather than encouragement! And remember too, that a little thought; a lot of care; and a good measure of self-control will prolong your horse's working life and keep him sound in wind and limb better than all the pills and potions in the medicine cupboard put together!*

THE GALLOP

1. <u>OUTSIDE</u> HIND LEG

2. <u>INSIDE</u> HIND ··· QUICKLY FOLLOWED BY ··· 3. <u>OUTSIDE</u> FORELEG

4. LASTLY··· <u>INSIDE</u> FORELEG

ABOUT PIPPA AND PETER

8 · *Reining Back*

When Pippa returned from the Pony Club Camp we asked her to come back once more with Peter to the circular drive round our front lawn, for there was still one more lesson yet to be learnt—how to ask Peter to step backwards when required.

It was a lesson that we had intentionally left till last, partly because it is undoubtedly the hardest one to ACHIEVE CORRECTLY, and partly because the rider's whole object should at all times be to aim for straight, free and forward movement. To attempt to 'rein back' too early may therefore help to destroy just that which one hopes to attain.

So we had waited until the very end and then had come back again to the garden before we attempted to explain to Pippa how to ask Peter to walk backward instead of forwards!

But 'walk backwards' is an incorrect term, because in reality we ask the horse to TROT BACK. For 'reining back' is, just like 'The Trot', a pace of two-time—ONE, TWO—Step-back, with first ONE DIAGONAL PAIR OF LEGS coming down together and then opposite numbers go back in unison.

There is, however, one great difference from 'The Trot'.

As the horse trots, for one split-second, invisible to the naked eye, there is a moment when he virtually bounces in the air—a moment of 'suspension' as it is called—when he jumps from one diagonal to the other.

To her great delight and thanks to her much improved riding, Pippa is invited to take a young pony to the Pony Club Camp.

David Tamplin

David Tamplin

Although the pony is strange to her she manages to keep a good position in the saddle and as a result his manners and education soon show signs of improvement.

Here you can see them joining in class work together.

David Tamplin

David Tamplin

And here both are enjoying expert tuition over the jumps.

(In her new position Pippa finds jumping a real pleasure instead of a somewhat alarming hazard! With the result that her pony has a feeling of real confidence too and willingly does his level best to get over!)

And so we say good-bye to Pippa and Peter as away they ride, happy, safe and confident in one another's company, in perfect tune and harmony together.

Richard Hammonds

Off they go into the distance determined to follow and explore that long road to 'more advanced riding' which, as they will soon discover, is so enthralling because it has no ending.

Richard Hammonds

Reining Back

Whereas to 'rein back' there is no moment of 'suspension', he just strides backward, his diagonal pair of legs moving slowly into place.

But how to make him do this? Once again, IT IS NOT DONE BY PULLING HIM BACK WITH THE REINS.

On the contrary, we asked Pippa to cast her mind back (and perhaps you would like once more to turn back the pages to one of the first lessons when Pippa learnt how to press Peter up, and into, a still, or 'unyielding rein' to produce 'flexion' and teach him to stop).

Now we want to PUSH the horse once again right up to that 'closed door', that STILL, FIRM and UNYIELDING rein.

But this time INSTEAD OF ALLOWING THAT REIN TO YIELD as we feel him beginning to relax his jaw, the rider must HOLD THE REIN FIRM AND CONTINUE TO PUSH THE HORSE STILL HARDER AND MORE DEFINITELY UP, AND INTO IT. So that he has no alternative as he finds he cannot simply 'stop'—but to BACK AWAY FROM IT.

As in everything else, patient practice is needed WITHOUT A SUGGESTION OF FORCE—until the horse tumbles to what is wanted and will obediently step back.

As this movement is ENTIRELY UNNATURAL TO HIM we must take care NEVER TO ASK for, or to expect more than one step backwards at a time to begin with; and as soon as he has done this, he must be praised, rewarded and QUICKLY SENT ON AGAIN. For the last thing we wish him to acquire is a taste for proceeding backwards!

Soon, if these instructions, like all the others that have gone before, have been intelligently and faithfully carried out, the horse will begin to understand and obey this command and step back any reasonable number of steps required of him (NEVER MORE THAN THREE TO FOUR SHOULD BE ASKED) without fluster or flurry, keeping as he should in a dead straight line even though such a request be foreign to his nature.

But 'reining back' is an advanced movement and should never be attempted nor taught until the rider himself has really progressed satisfactorily to this final stage in his more advanced riding, and the horse, too, has become reasonably suppled; well behaved; obedient; and his head correctly 'positioned' by endless properly regulated work at the walk.

So Pippa, having reached this happy goal, was recalled to the garden again to add this final and finishing touch. Though not often would Peter be asked to perform this feat, which was unnatural to him and a strain and effort for him to carry out.

Instead, Pippa continued to glory in his gentle obedience as they rode out along the lanes and across the fields together, both enjoying to the full each other's company, having reached the perfect harmony of complete trust and mutual understanding brought about by hard work and practice; moulded and blended together by the basic knowledge and understanding of the principles of more advanced riding; and liberally sprinkled with those essential ingredients—a little love, real friendship, great patience and true co-operation.

Some people refer to it all as elementary Dressage!

YOUR LESSON

LEARNING TO REIN BACK CORRECTLY

Last of all, and perhaps most difficult to execute properly, is 'The Rein Back'.

It is a two-time pace, which exactly resembles 'The Trot', when two diagonally opposite legs stride back in pairs together.

The only difference is that in 'The Rein Back' there is no spring—or 'moment of suspension' as it is called—as in 'The Trot'.

Off Fore and Near Hind . . . move back together.

Near Fore and Off Hind . . . stride back together.

One . . . Two.

Step . . . Back.

But to ask your horse to do this you DO NOT *just try to haul him back by tugging at the reins!*

Instead, cast your mind back, turn back the pages and study once more the directions given for asking your horse to 'Stop' correctly.

If you remember, you must push him UP *and* INTO a REIN THAT DOES NOT YIELD. *That is to say, a still rein that does not give* UNTIL *he has stopped. Then, when he is standing quite still, you* DO RELAX *that rein as his reward for obedience.*

When you want him to 'Rein Back' you do exactly the same thing. You still PUSH HIM FORWARDS *with all the strength at your command, again into that unyielding rein. But this time you must continue to* HOLD THAT REIN STILL—*keep the barrier up*

99

in fact—until, being unable to go farther forward, he soon realizes that there is nothing for it but to proceed backwards instead!

In order to help him, instead of sitting down hard as you do when asking him to stop and 'Halt', just raise your weight slightly in the saddle. This will appreciably lighten his load and make it easier for him to 'Rein Back' willingly.

But although it may all sound quite simple, in reality it is hard indeed to get a horse to step back quietly, CALMLY, *in smooth time, at steady pace, and above all in a dead straight line; and for this reason it is a movement best not attempted until your riding has indeed improved appreciably.*

REIN BACK

1. OFF FORE AND NEAR HIND BACK TOGETHER.

2. NEAR FORE AND OFF HIND BACK TOGETHER.